150 SECRETS FROM "THE INSIDE"

# Fine Dining

## PRISON COOKBOOK

### Troy Traylor

## Freebird Publishers

www.FreebirdPublishers.com

## Freebird Publishers

Box 541, North Dighton, MA 02764
Info@FreebirdPublishers.com
www.FreebirdPublishers.com

Copyright © 2019
Fine Dining Prison Cookbook
By Troy Traylor

All Freebird Publishers titles, imprints and distributed lines are available
at special quantity discounts for bulk purchases for sales promotions,
premiums, fundraising educational or institutional use.

ISBN-13: 978-0-9980361-9-9

Printed in the United States of America

This book is dedicated to
Madeline Emma Traylor,
Troy Neal Traylor, Jr.,
and all of my support team.

*I love each and every one of you!*

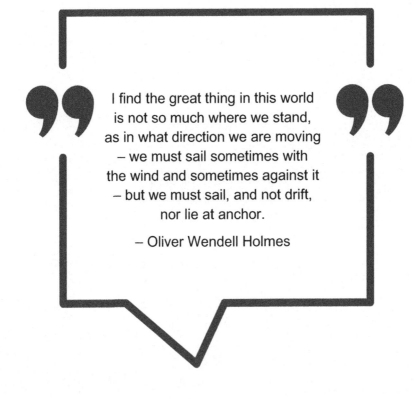

I find the great thing in this world
is not so much where we stand,
as in what direction we are moving
– we must sail sometimes with
the wind and sometimes against it
– but we must sail, and not drift,
nor lie at anchor.

– Oliver Wendell Holmes

# Acknowledgments

I would like to acknowledge the extraordinary debt I owe to all that contributed to this cookbook. I would not have been able to get my work done without the continual support and visions from each of you. This book is the way it is because of your ideas, encouragement, and belief in me and my dreams. The following is a list of some of these people. I thank and pray for each of you daily – may peace and love fill your hearts.

*Danny & Bonnie Cantrell*: I could never thank you enough for always believing in me and my dreams. You have been active in my life every step of the way. Even in the darkest of times you never gave up. When I needed emotional, spiritual, and financial support, you freely gave. You were both selfless when it comes to me, and I love you both dearly.

*Ms. Kelsey Eiland*: I am so grateful to you for choosing me to correspond with. You have freely shared with me and always went that extra mile. You have believed in me and encouraged me throughout this book-writing project. Knowing you fills me with joy and warmth. I could never re-pay you for treating me like a human being. I trust you have a reward awaiting you.

*Mrs. Jessica Hawkey*: Never in my life have I ever met anyone as dedicated and passionate as you are. You believe in change and making a difference in others' lives, and that is just what you do. Since corresponding with you I have grown a great deal. You have helped me to recognize that there is light at the end of my tunnel. Because of you, I now know the meaning of unconditional love, and I am filled with encouragement with your every letter. I am blessed to have you on my team and proud to call you my friend.

*Sister Kay, Sister Jennifer, and Brother Josh*: My thanks and respect goes out to each of you. You have shown and shared an abundance of love with me. You have led me to the Truth and have been a guide every step of the way. Our Father lives through you and my gratitude cannot be measured. God bless you, your families, and your ministry.

*Soul Sisters and all group members*: A special thanks goes out to each of you for your willingness to share my letter and gather recipes. I also thank you for remembering me when I felt forgotten. It brings a smile to my face just to know you care. It is safe to say that men/women all around the globe join in with me on these thanks.

*Mrs. Kim King*: My new friend that I look forward to corresponding with. You encourage me with your letters and encourage me to share my faith with you. I am inspired by you and thank God for you.

*Ms. Natasha Hickox*: Your willingness to forgive brings me life. I can never express in words my appreciation. I will spend the rest of this lifetime trying to prove my sincerity to you. May God fill you with His peace, love, and happiness.

*Ms. Madeline Traylor*: I am very proud to know you are my daughter. You have taken your struggles in life to become very strong and focused. You are proof that to accomplish things few people can accomplish; you have to do things few people are willing to do. Always remember that every day may not be good, but there is something good in every day. I love you more than you may ever know.

Now to the list of countless inmates and friends of inmates that have taken the time to share recipes and ideas with me. I have listed each of you in alphabetical order. My sincere appreciation goes out to you all. May this book encourage and inspire you to pursue your dreams. Thank you and know I am praying for you:

*John Black, WA*  
*Blair Blanchotto, MS*  
*Charlie Buckland, MD*  
*Marty Burns, TX*  
*Christopher Camden, TX*  

*James Campbell Jr., OH*  
*Kendall Hartl-Cantu, TX*  
*John Clarke, TX*  
*Daniel Cortez, TX*  
*Robert Dawson, WA*

Eric Decker ,IA
James Dickerson, CO
Carlos Espinoza, TX
Gary Farlow, NY
Joseph Garcia, TX
Darnell Gilyard, TX
Ashley Glass, ID
Scott Golden, TX
Benito Gutierrez, NY
Thomas Hall, TX
David Harris, TX
Robert Henderson, TX
Michael Henry, MD
Robbie Hickox, TX
Howard Jenkins, TX
Harry Katz, CO
Chris Killman, TX
Bob Leach, TX
Joseph Linden, TX
Roy Lopez, CA
Gilbert Martinez, TX
Robert McKinney, MD
Don Meyers, TX
Johnathan Might, MD
Vernon Miller, TX
Terry Millican, TX
Jesus Morales, TX

Kennegh Odem, TX
Tom Orton, NY
Robert Patnoude, CO
Sherry Perez, CO
Darnell Pickett, TX
Steve Pierce, CO
Dusty Rhodes, TX
Ernest Riley, CO
Chad Ritchie, ID
Uriel Rodriguez, NY
William Rowland, TX
Rene Sanchez, ID
Jeffery Schultz, NY
Paul Scoles, CO
Marty Snow, TX
Mark Switzer, TX
Isidro Teran, TX
Troy Traylor, Jr., MD
Troy Traylor, Sr., TX
Unknown writer, Unknown state.
Michelle Vargas,TX
Francisco Villela, TX
Tammy Wise, ID
Jason Whitman, State unknown
Donald Whycliff, IA

# Did You Know

… over 2.2 million people are currently in U.S. jails or prisons.

… the incarcerated population in the U.S. is more than the entire population of the state of New Mexico.

… the U.S. has the highest prison population in the entire world (with the exception of countries that cannot be verified, like North Korea).

… half of the world's prison population of approximately 9 million people is held in the U.S., Russia, or China.

… over 2.7 million children in the U.S. have a parent behind bars.

… there are over 5,000 jails and prisons in the U.S.

… there are more jails than colleges in the U.S.

… the U.S. prison population has more than quadrupled since the early 1980s: when mandatory minimum sentencing laws for drugs when into effect.

… about half of the inmates in federal prisons are serving time for non-violent drug offenses.

… federal law currently requires a mandatory minimum sentence of five years for a first-time, non-violent drug offense.

… approximately 60 percent of federal drug offenders are subject to mandatory minimum sentences.

… the average annual cost to incarcerate one inmate in federal prison is approximately $29,000.

… incarceration costs taxpayers almost $70 billion annually.

… state spending on corrections has grown about 300 percent in just the past 20 years.

… the Smarter Sentencing Act would save taxpayers nearly $24 billion over the next 20 years.

# Preface

My goal is to create and share a remarkable cookbook that will feel like you have just encountered a wonderful friend that you haven't seen in years and you set off together on a culinary journey. With 150 recipes that are far-ranging and delicious, you will learn to take a few common ingredients and make dining easy. With these "secrets from the inside," I hope to bring new creations, new ideas, and new – as we say – "hookups."

There is nothing more challenging than trying something new and meeting scores of enthusiastic people along the way. You can add your own ideas along the way, and you will fall in love with the results you produce. If you're someone who hates the long lines in a hot chow hall, you will be delighted with this dazzling collection of recipes.

This cookbook is about joy, passion, and thrill – joy of cooking; passion of eating; thrill of discovering something you hadn't known existed before. It offers the cure-all for any craving, as well as any appetite.

All these ingredients can be purchased at almost any unit commissary, and if you find yourself without something, don't be afraid to substitute and create your own flavor.

I have been blessed with recipes from all around the globe by countless individuals and hope to share them all around the globe with countless others. I just; cannot express my gratitude to each of you that contributed to this book. I am forever grateful.

Most of you don't know me, and will never meet me in person; however, once you've dipped into this book, I hope you will want to know more about me and my creations. I predict you'll want to dip again, and again, and again.

So, I ask you: Why do you think we cook the things we cook? Why do you think we crave the things we crave? What has the deepest effect on our culinary habits? Are we hungry? Bored?

Depressed? Maybe it is our environment, or possibly what we saw on television last night. Whatever the reason(s) may be, you now have at your disposal the "cure all."

This is a cookbook with a difference. Every aspect of this book has brought me great joy and a deep appreciation for the many people that contributed time, recipes, encouragement, and financial assistance. With the accomplishment of such an amazing achievement in my life, words are just not enough to describe my level of appreciation. For the first time, in a long time, I felt like I was treated like a friend, a brother, and a human being.

May all be blessed in abundance by our Heavenly Father and Creator. Thank you for believing in me and my dreams. With much love and respect …

Yours truly,

Troy Neal Traylor, Sr.

# Table of Contents

# Special Months for the Foodie

*January:* National Hot Tea Month, National Oatmeal Month, National Soup Month, National Fat Free Living Month

*February:* National Chocolate Lovers Month, National Cherry Month, National Grapefruit Month, National Potato Lovers Month

*March:* National Noodle Month, National Flour Month, National Nutrition Month, National Peanut Month, National Sauce Month

*April:* National Florida Tomato Month, National Soft Pretzel Month, National Grilled Cheese Month, National Garlic Month

*May:* National Barbecue Month, National Beef Month, National Loaded Potato Month, National Egg Month, National Hamburger Month, National Salad Month, National Salsa Month

*June:* National Candy Month, National Dairy Month, National Fresh Fruit and Vegetables Month, National Iced Tea Month

*July:* National Hot Dog Month, National Baked Bean Month, National Culinary Arts Month, National Ice Cream Month, National Picnic Month, National Pickle Month

*August:* National Catfish Month, National Panini Month, National Peach Month, National Sandwich Month

*September:* National Chicken Month, National Honey Month, National Mushroom Month, National Papaya Month, National Potato Month, National Rice Month, National Biscuit Month

*October:* National Pumpkin Month, National Popcorn Poppin' Month, National Apple Month, National Cookbook Month

*November:* National Peanut Butter Lovers' Month, National Georgia Pecan Month, National Pepper Month

*December:* National Pear Month, National Egg Nog Month, National Fruit Cake Month

*Conduct yourselves accordingly!*

# Supplies Needed – Inside/Outside

| *Inside* | *Outside* |
| --- | --- |
| Large & Small Spread Bowls | Large & Small Mixing Bowls |
| 12-ounce Coffee mug/Insert Cup | Same/16-ounce thick plastic cup |
| Hot Pot | Coffee Kettle |
| Empty Peanut Butter Jar | Same |
| Large and Small Chip Bags | Same |
| Rice bags | Same |
| Old Newspaper | Same |
| Crème Cookie Trays | Oreo Cookie Trays |
| Plastic Trash Bags | Same |
| ID Card | Knife |
| Desire | Same |
| Patience | Same |
| Passion | Same |
| Appetite | Same |
| Commissary Spoon | Tablespoon & Teaspoon |

**Helpful Hints**: Sizes of ingredients will vary slightly from state to state. When using liquids in recipes, especially sweets, it is best to use a little liquid at a time until you're familiar with the cooking process.

"Drying times" are all estimates. This varies due to the season and the temperature inside the building. Name brands can also affect drying times.

Anytime you are cooking in a hot pot, and using chip bags to cook in, it is best to double the bag so that water does not leak in. Rice bags are typically the best for cooking in.

For those of you that are on the outside and want to try some of our creations, you may not have a hot pot or coffee pot. You can cheat and use a microwave or stove. You will end up with the same results.

Finally, do not be afraid to substitute or add your own personal touch. Each person has different taste.

Have fun preparing and sharing. If ever possible, I would love to hear your thoughts on these recipes. I am also interested in collecting personal and family recipes for a future project.

May the Lord keep you and your loved ones safe.

# Understanding Food Components

*Proteins*: Composed of amino acids, are essential to good nutrition. They build, maintain, and repair the body. The best sources of proteins are eggs, milk, fish, meat, poultry, soybeans, and nuts. High-quality proteins, such as eggs, meat, or fish, supply all eight amino acids needed in a diet. Plant-sourced foods can be combined to meet the body's protein needs as well.

*Fats*: Provide energy by furnishing calories to the body. They also help the body absorb vitamins A, D, E, and K. The best sources of polyunsaturated and monounsaturated fats are vegetable/plant oils and nuts. Concentrated sources of saturated fats are meats, cheese, butter, cream, egg yolks, and lard.

*Carbohydrates*: These are the most important source of energy for the body. The digestive system changes carbohydrates into glucose, which the body uses for energy for cells, tissues, and organs. The body stores extra sugar in the liver and muscles. The best sources for carbs are grains, legumes, potatoes, vegetables, and fruits.

*Fiber*: This is the portion of plant foods that our bodies cannot digest. There are two basic types of fiber – insoluble and soluble. Insoluble fibers help move food materials through the digestive tract; soluble fibers tend to slow them down. Both types absorb water, thus preventing and treating constipation. Soluble fibers may also be helpful in reducing blood cholesterol levels. The best sources of fiber are beans, bran, fruits, whole grains, and vegetables.

*Water*: Dissolves and transports other nutrients throughout the body, aiding in the processes of digestion, absorption, circulation, and excretion. It also helps regulate body temperature.

# Vitamins

*Vitamin A*: Promotes good eyesight; helps keep skin and mucous membranes resistant to infection. The best sources of vitamin A are liver, sweet potatoes, carrots, kale, cantaloupe, turnip greens, collard greens, broccoli, and fortified milk.

*Vitamin $B_1$*: (thiamine) prevents beriberi. This vitamin is essential to carbohydrate metabolism and nervous system health. Best sources of thiamine are eggs, enriched bread and flour, nuts, seeds, organ meats, and whole grains.

*Vitamin $B_2$*: (riboflavin) protects the skin, mouth, eyes, and mucous membranes. The vitamin is essential to growth, red blood cell production, and energy metabolism. The best sources of riboflavin are dairy products, meat, poultry, broccoli, spinach, eggs, and nuts.

*Vitamin $B_6$*: (pyridoxine) is important in the regulation of the central nervous system and in protein metabolism. The best sources of $B_6$ are whole grains, meat, fish, nuts, avocado, and bananas.

*Vitamin $B_{12}$*: (cobalamin) is needed to form red blood cells. The best sources of $B_{12}$ are meat, shellfish, poultry, eggs, and dairy products.

*Niacin*: Maintains health of skin, nerves, and the digestive system. The best sources for niacin are poultry, nuts, fish, and eggs.

*Folic acid*: (folacin) is required for new cell formation, growth, reproduction, and for important chemical reactions in body cells. It is best found in leafy green vegetables, fruits, dried beans, peas, nuts, enriched bread, and cereal.

Other B vitamins include biotin and pantothenic acid.

*Vitamin C*: (ascorbic acid) maintains collagen, a protein necessary for the formation of skin, ligaments, and bones. Helps heal wounds and mends fractures. It is best obtained in citrus fruits and juices, cantaloupe, broccoli, Brussels sprouts, potatoes, sweet potatoes, and cabbage.

*Vitamin D*: This is important for bone development. The best sources for vitamin D are sunlight, milk products, tuna, salmon, and oysters.

*Vitamin E*: (tocopherol) helps protect red blood cells. The best places to find vitamin E are vegetable oils, wheat germ, whole grains, eggs, peanuts, margarine, and green leafy vegetables.

*Vitamin K*: This is necessary for formation of prothrombin, which helps blood to clot. Its best dietary sources are green leafy vegetables and tomatoes. (K is also made by intestinal bacteria.)

# Minerals

*Calcium*: Works with phosphorus to build and maintain bones and teeth. It is best found in dairy products and leafy green vegetables.

*Phosphorus*: Main function is in the formation of bones and teeth, but it performs more functions than any other mineral and plays a part in nearly every chemical reaction in the body. Its best sources are cheese, milk, meats, poultry, fish, and tofu.

*Iron*: This is necessary for the formation of myoglobin, a reservoir of oxygen for muscle tissue, and hemoglobin, which transports oxygen within blood. It is best found in lean meats, beans, green leafy vegetables shellfish, and whole grains.

Other minerals include chloride, chromium, cobalt, copper, fluoride, iodine, magnesium, molybdenum, potassium, selenium, sulfur, and zinc.

# Did You Know

… chocolate was once used as currency.

… the most expensive pizza in the world cost $12,000.00 and takes 72 hours to make.

... there is an amusement park in Tokyo that offers Raw Horse Flesh flavored ice cream.

… Coca-Cola was invented in the U.S in 1885 by John Stith Pemberton.

… the oldest evidence for soup is from 6,000 B.C. and calls for hippopotamus and sparrow meat.

… pound cake got its name from its original recipe, which called for a pound each of butter, eggs, sugar, and flour.

… one of the most popular pizza toppings in Brazil is green peas.

… the average ear of corn has an even number of rows. Usually 16.

… apples belong to the rose family, as do pears and plums.

… tea bags were created accidentally. Tea bags were originally used to send tea out as samples.

… Pringles once had a lawsuit against them trying to prove that they weren't really potato chips.

… a ripe cranberry will bounce like a rubber ball.

… Central Appalachia's tooth decay problem is referred to as "Mountain Dew mouth," because of the beverage's popularity in the region.

… castoreum, which is used as vanilla flavoring in candles, baked goods, and more … is actually a secretion from the anal glands of beavers. (Did you really want to know that?)

# Healthy Eating

Healthy eating patterns will include a variety from the following food groups:

*Vegetables* from the five subgroups: dark green, red and orange, legumes (beans and peas), starchy, and other.

*Fruits*: especially whole fruits.

*Grains*: at least half of which should be whole grains. Choose refined grains that are enriched.

*Fat-Free or low-fat dairy*: Including milk, yogurt, and cheese. Those who cannot or choose not to consume dairy should eat foods, such as fortified soy beverages, that provide the same nutrients.

*A variety of protein foods*: Including seafood, lean meats and poultry, eggs, nuts, seeds, and soy products. Legumes (beans and peas) can be considered vegetables or proteins but should be counted in one group only.

*Oils*: such as corn oil and olive oil, are fats that are usually liquid at room temperature because of their higher percentage of unsaturated fatty acids. Oils should replace solid fats where possible.

*Potassium, dietary fiber, calcium, and vitamin D* are among the nutrients under consumed in American diets, which affects public health. The under consumption of iron by young children and women who could become or are pregnant is also a concern.

# Dietary Components to Limit

* Less than 2,300 mg per day of sodium. Adults with prehypertension and hypertension may benefit from consuming less than 1,500 mg of sodium per day.

* Less than 10% of daily calories from saturated fats: replace with monounsaturated and polyunsaturated fats.

* Less than 10% of daily calories from added sugars.

* As little as possible of trans fats and dietary cholesterol.

* Alcohol in moderation, if at all – up to one drink per day for women and two drinks per day for men.

# Section I:
# A Few Tasty Drinks

# Convict Latté

Contributed by Troy Traylor

### Ingredients
1 Milky Way candy bar
3 tablespoons hot chocolate mix
6 tablespoons French vanilla cappuccino
1 coffee mug hot water

### Directions
Place Milky Way in a hot pot and allow to fully melt (approximately 30 minutes). Once melted, combine all ingredients in your coffee mug and stir well. (An optional tablespoon of peanut butter is also good.)

Keep away from people who try to belittle your ambitions.
Small people always do that,
but the really great make you feel that you, too,
can become great.
– Mark Twain

# Fireball Express-O

Contributed by Kennegh Odem

### Ingredients
8 tablespoons cappuccino
3 fireball candies
1 (1 ounce) mint stick
1 coffee mug hot water

### Directions
Place the cappuccino in a coffee mug. Crush up the mint stick and fireballs and add these ingredients to your cup. Now pour in your hot water and stir until it everything is dissolved. This is a really good way to begin any day.

 In every adversity there are the seeds
of an equal or greater opportunity.
– Clement Stone

# Reese's Pieces Peanut Butter Cup Drink

Contributed by Jason Whitman

## Ingredients
3 heaping tablespoons hot chocolate
1 coffee mug hot water
1 tablespoon peanut butter
1 bag of Reese's Pieces

## Directions
In your coffee mug combine all the ingredients and mix until all is dissolved. That's it, drink up and enjoy.

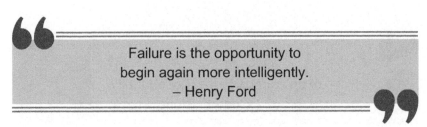

Failure is the opportunity to
begin again more intelligently.
– Henry Ford

# Salted Soda

Contributed by Troy Traylor

### Ingredients
1/2 of a two-ounce bag of salted peanuts
1 twelve-ounce soda of your choice

### Directions
Add peanuts to an ice-cold
soda, wait 5 minutes, stir a
bit, and "drink up." If you
have never tried this, you
will not believe the taste of
each!

More people fail from lack
of purpose than lack of talent.
– Billy Sunday

# Special Days for the Foodie

January
(1st): National Black Eyed Pea Day
(2nd): National Buffet Day, National Cream Puff Day
(3rd): National Chocolate Covered Cherry Day
(4th): National Spaghetti Day
(5th): National Whipped Cream Day
(6th): National Shortbread Day, National Bean Day
(7th): National Tempura Day
(8th): National English Toffee Day
(9th): National Apricot Day
(10th): National Bittersweet Chocolate Day
(11th): National Hot Toddy Day, National Milk Day
(12th): National Marzipan Day, National Curried Chicken Day
(13th): National Gluten-Free Day; National Peach Melba Day
(14th): National Hot Pastrami Sandwich Day
(15th): National Bagel Day, National Fresh Squeezed Juice Day
(16th): International Hot and Spicy Food Day
(17th): National Hot Buttered Rum Day
(18th): National Gourmet Coffee Day, Peking Duck Day
(19th): National Popcorn Day
(20th): National Butter-crunch Day, National Cheese Lover's Day
(21st): National Granola Bar Day
(22nd): National Southern Food Day
(23rd): National Pie Day, National Rhubarb Pie Day
(24th): National Peanut Butter Day
(25th): National Irish Coffee Day
(26th): National Peanut Brittle Day
(27th): National Chocolate Cake Day
(28th): National Blueberry Pancake Day
(29th): National Corn Chip Day
(30th): National Croissant Day
(31st): National Hot Chocolate Day

# Section II:
# **Condiments, Dips, & Creamy Spreads**

# Buffalo Chicken Dip

Contributed by Gary Farlow

### Ingredients
1 eight-ounce package old fashioned cream cheese
1 coffee mug old fashioned ranch or blue cheese dressing
1 coffee mug shredded food express mozzarella cheese
4 five-ounce packages Back Country buffalo chicken with sauce
2 three-ounce bags of Doritos

### Directions

Allow cream cheese to soften, and then combine with the ranch or blue cheese dressing. Whip until all is smooth. Add the cheese and chicken to the dressing mixture, including sauce out of the chicken packages. Place bowl in a microwave and heat just long enough to get the mixture bubbling hot (about 3-4 minutes). Stir well. Enjoy with your Doritos (or crackers).

More often than not,
when something looks like
it's the absolute end,
it is really the beginning.
– Charles Swindoll

# Fireball Mustard

Contributed by Troy Traylor

**Ingredients**
4 fireball candies
1 fourteen-ounce bottle of mustard
1 tablespoon hot water
5 heaping tablespoons salad dressing

**Directions**
Crush and melt fireball candies in the hot water. Combine all ingredients in a spread bowl and mix well. Spoon the mixture back into the bottle or jar. You have to try this one to appreciate it.

To succeed, it is necessary
to accept the world as it is and rise above it.
– Michael Korda

# Lemon-Pepper Mayo

Contributed by Troy Traylor

### Ingredients
1 fifteen-ounce bottle salad dressing
2 packages lemon lime electrolyte (0.34 ounces each)
1 teaspoon hot water
1½ teaspoons black pepper

### Directions
Pour salad dressing into a spread bowl and dissolve electrolyte in the hot water. Combine all ingredients and mix well. Spoon back into the bottle or jar. This mayo really helps bring a meal to life! Try on potatoes.

* Each package of electrolyte is equal to 1 tablespoon electrolyte or 4 tablespoons Kool-Aid.

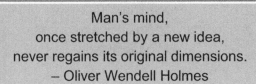
Man's mind,
once stretched by a new idea,
never regains its original dimensions.
– Oliver Wendell Holmes

# Mc B's Dip & More

Contributed by Troy Traylor

**Ingredients**
4 packages ranch dressing (1.5 ounce each) *
2 two-ounce packages of cream cheese*
1/4 package lemon lime electrolyte (.34 ounce each)*

**Directions**
In a small bowl or coffee mug, combine all ingredients and mix well. Can be eaten on fish dishes, burritos, and tortilla chips.

* Each package of ranch dressing is equal to 2 tablespoons.
* Each package of cream cheese is equal to 4 tablespoons.
* Each package of electrolyte is equal to 1 tablespoon electrolyte or 4 tablespoons Kool-Aid.

Self-trust is the first
secret of success.
– Ralph Waldo Emerson

# Mc B's Hot Mustard

Contributed by Troy Traylor

**Ingredients**

2 fireball candies

1 fourteen-ounce bottle mustard

2 tablespoons habanera sauce

1 teaspoon hot water

2 packages chili seasoning from Ramen

**Directions**

Crush and melt fireball candies in hot water. Now, using a large spread bowl, combine all the ingredients and stir well. Make sure all is mixed thoroughly. Spoon mixture back into the bottle or jar. This mustard is great on chicken meals and burritos.

Use what talents you possess;
the woods would be very
silent if no birds sang except
those that sang best.
– Henry Van Dyke

# Mc B's Sweet & Spicy Mustard

Contributed by Troy Traylor

### Ingredients
1 fourteen-ounce bottle mustard
2 packages chili seasoning from Ramen
2 packages lemon lime electrolyte (.34 ounce each) *
1 tablespoon hot water

### Directions
Pour mustard in a spread bowl and stir in chili seasoning. Dissolve electrolyte in the hot water and add to bowl. Stir until thoroughly mixed. Spoon mixture back into the bottle or jar. Enjoy this on just about any sandwich.

* Packages of electrolyte are equal to 1 tablespoon electrolyte or 4 tablespoons Kool-Aid.

To accomplish great things,
we must dream as
well as act.
– Anatle France

# Mc B's Twangy Mayo

Contributed by Troy Traylor

**Ingredients**
1 fifteen-ounce bottle salad dressing
1 teaspoon hot water
1 package orange electrolyte (.34 ounce)*

**Directions**
Pour all salad dressing into a spread bowl. Dissolve electrolyte in the hot water and stir into salad dressing. Once all is mixed well, spoon it back into the jar. This will make a tremendous difference on your favorite sandwich.

* Packages of electrolyte are equal to 1 tablespoon electrolyte or 4 tablespoons Kool-Aid.

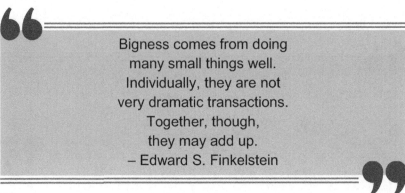

Bigness comes from doing
many small things well.
Individually, they are not
very dramatic transactions.
Together, though,
they may add up.
– Edward S. Finkelstein

# Penn-Style Sandwich Spread

Contributed by Mark Switzer

### Ingredients
1 fifteen-ounce jar salad dressing
1 nine-ounce dill pickle
1/2 bottle onion flakes (a 1.75-ounce bottle) *
1/3 bottle ketchup (a 20-ounce bottle)
2 jalapeno peppers (singles – 1.3 ounces each)
1 tablespoon hot water

### Directions
Use a large spread bowl and combine salad dressing and ketchup. Mix well. Dice up pickle and jalapeno peppers into tiny pieces and add to bowl. Hydrate onion flakes with 1 tablespoon hot water and add to mixture. Spoon mixture back into 2 jars for a quick, fast, and delicious sandwich spread.

* Onion flakes in this recipe would be equal to approximately 3 tablespoons.

Craft against vice I
will apply.
– William Shakespeare,
*Measure for Measure*

# Special Days for the Foodie

## February
(1st): National Cake Pops Day, National Dark Chocolate Day

(2nd): National Tater Tot Day

(3rd): National Carrot Cake Day

(4th): National Homemade Soup Day

(5th): World Nutella Day, National Frozen Yogurt Day

(6th): National Chopsticks Day

(7th): National Fettuccine Alfredo Day

(8th): National Molasses Bar Day, National Potato Lover's Day

(9th): National Bagels and Lox Day, National Pizza Day

(10th): National "Have a Brownie" Day

(11th): National Peppermint Patty Day

(12th): National Plum Pudding Day, National PB&J Day

(13th): National Tortellini Day, National "Italian Food" Day

(14th): National Cream-Filled Chocolates Day

(15th): National Gumdrop Day, National Chewing Gum Day

(16th): National Almond Day

(17th): National Cafe' Au Lait Day

(18th): National "Drink Wine" Day

(19th): National Chocolate Mint Day

(20th): National Cherry Pie Day, National Muffin Day

(21st): National Pancake Day, National Sticky Bun Day

(22nd): National Cook a Sweet Potato Day

(23rd): National Chili Day, National Banana Bread Day

(24th): National Tortilla Chip Day

(25th): National Chocolate-Covered Peanuts Day

(26th): National Pistachio Day

(27th): National Strawberry Day, National Kahlua Day

(28th): National Chocolate Souffle Day

(29th): National Frog Legs Day

# Section III:
# Side Dishes & Quick Snacks

# Cheese Puff Madness

Contributed by Troy Traylor

**Ingredients**
1 eleven-ounce bag Cheese Puffs
1 fifteen-ounce bottle sandwich spread

**Directions**
This is the easiest recipe you will find: Open the bag of Cheese Puffs and open the jar of sandwich spread. Dip each Cheese Puff one time. No double dipping allowed.

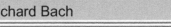

You are never given a
dream without also having
been given the power
to make it come true.
– Richard Bach

# Cheese Stuffed Jalapenos

Contributed by Troy Traylor

### Ingredients
1 coffee mug crushed cheese puffs
2 one-and-a-half-ounce packages ranch dressing*
6-8 jalapeno peppers (singles – 1.3 ounces each)

### Directions
Crush cheese puffs into a fine powder. In a cup or small spread bowl combine cheese puffs and ranch dressing. Mix well. Cut jalapeno peppers open length wise and de-seed. Stuff pepper halves with cheese puffs mixture. Cut up some typing paper into squares big enough to wrap each pepper halve in. Roll up each pepper, place all in a rice bag, and set down in a hot pot to heat for 2 hours. These make a nice addition to any meal.

* Packages of ranch dressing are equal to 2 tablespoons each.

Laziness grows on people;
it begins in cobwebs
and ends in iron chains.
– M. Hale

# Country D's Rice

Contributed by Donald Whycliff

### Ingredients
1 twelve-ounce Big Red soda
1 eight-ounce package Mexican beef
1/2 of an eight-ounce bag of instant rice
1/3 of a nine-ounce dill pickle
1 two-and-three-quarter-ounce bag of pork skins
1 package beef seasoning from Ramen
1 package chili seasoning from Ramen
1/2 teaspoon black pepper
2 tablespoons squeeze cheese
2 tablespoons salad dressing

### Directions
Open soda and place in a hot pot, along with the package of Mexican beef. Heat both until hot. Once soda is hot, combine soda and rice in a large spread bowl (or in the rice bag). Cover bowl tightly, wrap in a towel, and let cook for 10 minutes. While waiting for rice to cook, cut up pickle and lightly crush pork skins. Once rice is cooked, combine all remaining ingredients and stir well. If any liquid remains in rice after it is cooked, do not drain. You can eat this as is, on snack crackers, or in flour tortillas. This is how a country boy does it.

> Where we love is home –
> home that our feet may leave,
> but not our hearts.
> – Oliver Wendell Holmes

# Crazy Corn

Contributed by Marty Burns

### Ingredients
1 four-ounce serving corn from tray
1 tablespoon salad dressing
2 tablespoons parmesan cheese
1/2 teaspoon hot sauce

### Directions
In a small spread bowl mix all the ingredients together and eat
with your favorite spread. Just like home.

In the middle of difficulty lies opportunity.
– Albert Einstein

# Fat Boys Sandwich

Contributed by Jeffery Shultz

**Ingredients**
1 jalapeno pepper (single 1.3 ounce)
1/4 of a five-ounce summer sausage
1 cinnamon raisin bagel (single 2.75 ounce)
1 tablespoon chili garlic sauce
1 tablespoon squeeze cheese

**Directions**
Dice up jalapeno pepper and summer sausage. Separate bagel into 2 pieces and spread chili garlic sauce on bottom half. Add summer sausage on top of the chili garlic sauce then add the jalapeno pepper. Top off with the squeeze cheese and the other half of the bagel. Place on a napkin and put in a microwave for 45 seconds on high. I know this sounds crazy, but what a combination it makes. If you have no microwave, place the bagel in a rice bag and set in a boiling hot pot for 15 minutes.

Avoid dishonest gain:
no price can recompense
the pangs of vice.
– Benjamin Franklin,
*Poor Richard's Almanack*

# Chicken Nuggets

Contributed by Dusty Rhodes

**Ingredients**
1 eight-ounce bag jalapeno chips
1 seven-ounce package chicken chunks
8 tablespoons hot water
1 three-ounce bag Salsa Verde chips
1 one-and-a-half-ounce package ranch dressing*
2 tablespoons BBQ sauce

**Directions**

Crush jalapeno chips into a fine powder. Do not drain chicken chunks. Shred chicken chunks and add to jalapeno chip bag, with the hot water. Knead well. Once kneaded, divide mixture into 8 equal parts and roll into balls. Flatten these out a bit, just to get your nugget shape. Now crush the Salsa Verde chips and coat each nugget thoroughly. Carefully place these 8 pieces in a rice bag and place bag in a hot pot to heat for 2 hours. While waiting, combine the ranch dressing and BBQ sauce together in a small bowl or cup. Mix well. This is your sauce. A fairly easy recipe, which renders remarkable results.

* Package of ranch dressing is equal to 2 tablespoons.

Good habits result from
resisting temptation.
– Ancient Proverb

# Jail Mix Trail Mix

Contributed by Troy Traylor

## Ingredients
2 three-ounce spicy vegetable Ramen
1 two-ounce package salted peanuts
1/4 coffee mug sunflower seeds
1 package regular size M & M's

## Directions
Crush Ramen noodles and put in a clean, large chip bag. Add just 1 seasoning package to bag. Now add remaining ingredients and shake well. To make an entire bag, just double the ingredients. This is the fastest recipe in Texas. Leave other seasoning for another recipe.

> We can't solve problems by using the same kind of thinking we used when we created them.
> – Mary Sarton

# Meaty Scalloped Potatoes

Contributed by Troy Traylor

### Ingredients
3/4 coffee mug instant milk
1 two-ounce package cream cheese*
1 seven-ounce package chicken chunks
1 coffee mug hot water
1/3 of a sixteen-ounce bottle of squeeze cheese
1/2 of an eight-ounce bag of jalapeno chips

### Directions
In a large spread bowl combine instant milk and hot water. Stir until all is dissolved. After mixing, add cream cheese and squeeze cheese to the bowl. Mix thoroughly. Mixture will be on thick side. Drain and shred chicken chunks and add this to the bowl. Stir. Leave chips whole and in the bag. Now add the milk mixture to chip bag and lightly knead. Chips will soften. If too stiff, just add a little water. Place this bag in a hot pot to heat for 2 hours. Best to double bag so no water gets in. Stir occasionally. Again, if mixture gets too stiff add a little water. You want this to be thick and creamy. When cook time is up, pour all in your bowl and enjoy some fine dining!

*Package of cream cheese is equal to 4 tablespoons.

> Temptation rarely comes in working hours.
> It is in their leisure time that men are made or marred.
> – W. N. Taylor

# Nubs' Baked Potato

Contributed by William Rowland

**Ingredients**
1 eight-ounce bag jalapeno chips
1/3 coffee mug hot water
2 tablespoons squeeze cheese
1 eight-ounce bag BBQ chips
1 one-and-a-half-ounce package ranch dressing*

**Directions**
Crush all chips and combine in 1 large chip bag. Add hot water to bag and knead well. Water will absorb and chips will soften. Roll this mixture into your potato. Double bag and place bag in a hot pot for 1 hour. Once cook time is up, place potato in a spread bowl and top with ranch dressing and squeeze cheese. This is a great side dish with any meal. See recipe for a stuffed potato in the meal section.

*Package of ranch dressing is equal to 2 tablespoons.

Nothing is as certain as that the vices of leisure
are gotten rid of by being busy.
– Seneca (5 BC-65 AD),
*Moral Letters to Lucilius*, 64 AD

# Pickle Perfection

Contributed by James Dickerson

**Ingredients**
1 nine-ounce dill pickle
1 packet (.14 ounce) grape Kool-Aid

**Directions**
Cut up the pickle into slices, just as you would for a burger. Clean out an empty peanut butter jar and put all pickle slices in it. Add the Kool-Aid and the pickle juice to the jar. Shake until all the Kool-Aid dissolves. Allow this jar to sit for 2-3 days. Shake occasionally. You can use more or less Kool-Aid to adjust to your desired taste. All flavors of Kool-Aid can be used. Try lemon, for sure.

*Packet of Kool-Aid is equal to 2 tablespoons.

That which does not destroy me
makes me strong.
– Friedrich Nietzche

# Potato Salad Madness

Contributed by Marty Snow

**Ingredients**
1/2 of an eight-ounce bag of Shabang chips
3/4 of a nine-ounce dill pickle
1 hot pot of hot water
3½ tablespoons salad dressing
2 jalapeno peppers (1.3 ounce singles)
2 coffee mugs of four-cheese instant potatoes
2 tablespoons mustard
1 package chili seasoning from Ramen

**Directions**
Crush chips and dice jalapeno peppers and pickle. In a large spread bowl combine chips, instant potatoes, and hot water. Mix thoroughly. You want a stiff mixture. Make sure all is mixed well. Add remaining ingredients and mix again. Chips can be substituted with salt & vinegar.

> Don't flatter yourself that friendship authorizes you to say disagreeable things to your intimates. The nearer you come into relation with a person, the more necessary do tact and courtesy become. Except in cases of necessity, which are rare, leave your friend to learn unpleasant things from his enemies; they are ready enough to tell them.
> – Oliver Wendell Holmes

# Stuffed Pickle II

Contributed by Troy Traylor

**Ingredients**
2 nine-ounce dill pickles (any flavor)
1 five-ounce summer sausage
1/4 coffee mug instant rice
1 coffee mug hot water
1/2 coffee mug of Shabang chips
1 packet ranch dressing (1.5 ounce)

**Directions**

Using the handle of a spoon, dig out the inside of the pickles. Leave just skin and a little pickle inside. Also leave one end closed. Dice up summer sausage into tiny pieces. Combine your rice and hot water in a spread bowl, cover tightly, and allow to cook for 10-12 minutes. When rice is ready, drain any excess water and fluff up. Crush chips and place in the bowl with rice. Now add summer sausage and stir well. Stuff pickles with this mixture. Place both pickles in a rice bag and place bag in a hot pot to heat for 1 hour. The hotter the pot, the better. After cook time is up, place pickles in a spread bowl and top with ranch dressing.

*Package of ranch dressing is equal to 2 tablespoons.

Habit, if not resisted,
soon becomes necessity.
– Augustine

# Queso Fundido

Contributed by Gary Farlow

**Ingredients**
1 medium/large onion, diced
1 eleven-and-a-quarter-ounce Back Country chorizo
1 tablespoon Texas Pete hot sauce
2 tablespoons butter
2 four-ounce packages food express mozzarella cheese sticks
1 four-ounce Velveeta queso blanco
1 sixteen-ounce bag nacho chips*

**Directions**
In a microwave-safe bowl, combine onion, chorizo, and Texas Pete. Microwave on high for 2 minutes. In a separate dish, rub bottom and sides with 1 tablespoon of butter. Add mozzarella and queso blanco on top of buttered bowl with remaining tablespoon of butter on top of that. Microwave on high 2½ minutes, or until cheese begins to bubble. Remove  from microwave and top with chorizo mixture in center. Serve with your nacho chips. Feeds 2 hungry people.

*Nacho chips can be substituted with Doritos or tortilla chips.

Victory attained by violence is tantamount
to a defeat, for it is momentary.
– Mahatma Gandhi (1869-1948),
*Satyagraha Leaflet No. 13*,
May 13, 1919

# Special Days for the Foodie

March
(1st): National Peanut Butter Lover's Day
(2nd): National Banana Cream Pie Day
(3rd): National Cold Cuts Day, National Moscow Mule Day
(4th): National Pound Cake Day
(5th): National Cheese Doodle Day
(6th): National Oreo Day
(7th): National Cereal Day
(8th): National Peanut Cluster Day
(9th): National Meatball Day, National Crab Day
(10th): National Ranch Dressing Day
(11th): National "Eat Your Noodles" Day
(12th): National Milky Way Day
(13th): National Chicken Noodle Soup Day
(14th): National Potato Chip Day
(15th): National Peanut Lovers' Day
(16th): National Artichoke Heart Day
(17th): National Irish Food Day
(18th): National Sloppy Joe Day
(19th): National Oatmeal Cookie Day
(20th): National Ravioli Day
(21st): National Crunchy Taco Day
(22nd): National Water Day
(23rd): National Chips and Dip Day
(24th): National Cake Pop Day, National Tortilla Chip Day
(25th): National International Waffle Day
(26th): National Nougat Day, National Spinach Day
(27th): National World Whisky Day
(28th): National Black Forest Cake Day
(29th): National Chiffon Cake Day
(30th): National Hot Chicken Day
(31st): National Oysters on the Half Shell Day, National Clam Day

April

(1st): National Sourdough Bread Day

(2nd): National Peanut Butter and Jelly Day

(3rd): National Chocolate Mousse Day

(4th): National Cordon Bleu Day, International Carrot Day

(5th): Caramel Day, National Raisin & Spice Bar Day

(6th): National Caramel Popcorn Day, New Beer's Eve

(7th): National Coffee Cake Day, National Beer Day

(8th): National Empanada Day

(9th): National Chinese Almond Cookie Day

(10th): National Cinnamon Crescent Day

(11th): National Cheese Fondue Day

(12th): National Grilled Cheese Sandwich Day

(13th): National Peach Cobbler Day

(14th): National Pecan Day

(15th): National Glazed Ham Day

(16th): National Eggs Benedict Day, Day of the Mushroom

(17th): National Cheese ball Day, World Malbec (wine) Day

(18th): National Animal Crackers Day

(19th): National Rice Ball Day

(20th): National Pineapple Upside-down Cake Day

(21st): National Chocolate-Covered Cashews Day

(22nd): National Jelly Bean Day

(23rd): National Cherry Cheesecake Day, National Picnic Day

(24th): National Pigs-in-a-Blanket Day

(25th): National Crotilla* Day, National Zucchini Bread Day

(26th): National Pretzel Day

(27th): National Prime Rib Day

(28th): National Blueberry Pie Day

(29th): National Shrimp Scampi Day

(30th): National Oatmeal Cookie Day, National Raisin Day

*a cross between a croissant and a tortilla, introduced by Walmart

# Section IV:
# Gumbos & Chowder

# Fine Dining Gumbo

Contributed by Howard Jenkins

**Ingredients**
1 seven-ounce package chicken chunks
1 five-ounce summer sausage
1 three-and-a-half-ounce package mackerel
1 eleven-and-a-quarter-ounce package beef stew
2 jalapeno peppers (1.3 ounce singles)
1 eight-ounce bag jalapeno chips
3½ coffee mugs hot water
3/4 of an eight-ounce bag of instant rice
3 Ramen seasoning packets: 1/2 packet of beef, 1/2 packet of chicken, and 1 packet chili
1 two-and-three-quarter-ounce bag pork skins
1 sixteen-ounce bag tortilla chips (optional)

**Directions**
Shred chicken chunks and finely dice summer sausage. Drain mackerel. Dice jalapeno peppers and crush jalapeno chips. In a rice bag, combine chicken chunks, summer sausage, mackerel, beef stew, jalapeno peppers, chips, and one coffee mug hot water and mix well. Now place bag in a hot pot to cook for 3 hours. Stir occasionally. After 2 hours and 45 minutes combine rice, all seasonings, and remaining water, in a large spread bowl. Mix well and cover tightly until meat mixture is ready. Drain any excess water from rice. Pour meat mixture over rice and mix well. Now add pork skins and mix again. Cover for 5 minutes so pork skins soften. This is fine dining, for sure!

Creativity takes courage. – Henry Matisse

# Hearty Gumbo

Contributed by Troy Traylor

### Ingredients
1 eight-ounce bag jalapeno chips
1 eight-ounce package beef tips
1/2 of a twelve-ounce V-8 juice
4 flour tortillas
1 five-ounce summer sausage
1 eleven-and-a-quarter-ounce package beef stew
3 tablespoons squeeze cheese

### Directions

Crush up chips fairly well. Dice summer sausage and shred beef tips. Set aside flour tortillas and combine all remaining ingredients in a chip bag. Double bag and place in a hot pot to heat for 4 hours. Stir occasionally. When thoroughly cooked, pour into a large spread bowl. Tear up the flour tortillas and stir into the bowl. Additional seasoning is okay, but it is already seasoned well. Enjoy!

Far better it is to dare mighty things,
to win glorious triumphs,
even though checkered by failure,
then to take rank with those poor spirits,
who neither enjoy much nor suffer much,
because they live in the gray twilight
that knows neither victory nor defeat.
– Theodore Roosevelt

# Mackerel Chowder

Contributed by Paul Scoles

### Ingredients
1/2 coffee mug instant milk
1 four-ounce serving green beans
1/2 teaspoon onion powder
1 teaspoon onion flakes
4 two-ounce packages cream cheese
1 coffee mug hot water
1 four-ounce serving carrots
1 package chicken seasoning from Ramen
2 three-and-a-half-ounce packages mackerel
1 sleeve saltine crackers

### Directions
In a large spread bowl, combine instant milk and hot water. Mix until dissolved. Set the saltine crackers aside for a moment and combine all the remaining ingredients. Mix all well. Grab your crackers and enjoy this hot treat on a cold day. (Vegetables will come off a tray. Nice hook up for segregation.)

*Packages of cream cheese are equal to 4 tablespoons each.

Happiness is a butterfly,
which when pursued is always
just beyond your grasp, but which,
if you will sit down quietly,
may alight up you.
– Nathaniel Hawthorne
(1804-1864)

# Potato Beef Chowder

Contributed by Troy Traylor

**Ingredients**

1 large or 2 medium size potatoes

1/4 of a sixteen-ounce bottle of squeeze cheese

2 coffee mugs hot water

black pepper to taste

1 tablespoon onion powder

2 four-ounce servings broccoli from tray

3/4 coffee mug instant milk

1 five-ounce beef summer sausage

1 teaspoon garlic powder

1 three-ounce beef Ramen noodles

**Directions**

Cut up potatoes and broccoli and place all in a large spread bowl. In a small spread bowl, combine squeeze cheese, instant milk, and hot water. Mix until dissolved and mixture is creamy. Cut up summer sausage into small cubes, add to broccoli mixture, and combine with the cheese mixture, and seasonings. Mix well and place mixture in a large, 16-ounce chip bag. Double bag and place in a hot pot to cook for 1½ hours. Stir occasionally. About 30 minutes prior to cook time is complete, lightly crush Ramen and add it and the seasoning to the bag. Stir well and cook for the remaining 30 minutes.

Events of great consequence often
spring from trifling circumstances.
– Livy

# Tomato Vegetable Noodle Soup

Contributed by Troy Traylor

### Ingredients
1/2 of a twenty-ounce bottle ketchup
2 coffee mugs hot water
2 four-ounce servings mixed vegetables from tray
2 tablespoons butter
1 three-ounce chili Ramen noodles
black pepper to taste
1 sleeve saltine crackers

### Directions
In a large spread bowl, combine ketchup, hot water, vegetables, butter, Ramen noodles, and seasoning package. Stir well. Cover bowl tightly and allow to cook for 10 minutes. Add your pepper and break out the crackers. This recipe is also great for segregation offenders.

Nothing brings more pain than too much pleasure;
nothing more bondage than too much liberty.
– Benjamin Franklin

# Special Days for the Foodie

May

(1st): National Chocolate Parfait Day

(2nd): National Chocolate Truffle Day

(3rd): National Chocolate Custard Day, National Raspberry Tart Day,

(4th): National Candied Orange Peel Day, National Hoagie Day

(5th): National Enchilada Day (Happy Cinco de Mayo!)

(6th): National Crepe Suzette Day

(7th): National Roast Leg of Lamb Day

(8th): National Coconut Cream Pie Day

(9th): National Shrimp Day, National Foodies Day

(10th): National Liver and Onions Day

(11th): National "Eat What You Want" Day

(12th): National Nutty Fudge Day

(13th): National Apple Pie Day, National Fruit Cocktail Day

(14th): National Brioche Day, National Buttermilk Biscuit Day

(15th): National Chocolate Chip Day

(16th): National Barbecue Day

(17th): National Cherry Cobbler Day

(18th): National Cheese Soufflé Day, I love Reese's Day

(19th): National Devil's Food Cake Day

(20th): National Quiche Lorraine Day, National Pick Strawberries Day

(21st): National Strawberries and Cream Day

(22nd): National Vanilla Pudding Day

(23rd): National Taffy Day

(24th): National Escargot Day

(25th): National Brown-Bag-It Day, National Wine Day

(26th): National Blueberry Cheesecake Day

(27th): National Italian Beef Day, National Grape Popsicle Day

(28th): National Brisket Day

(29th): National Biscuit Day

(30th): National Mint Julep Day

(31st): National Macaroon Day

June

(1st): National Hazelnut Cake Day

(2nd): National Rocky Road Day, National Rotisserie Chicken Day

(3rd): National Chocolate Macaroon Day, National Egg Day

(4th): National Cheese Day

(5th): National Ketchup (Catsup) Day

(6th): National Gingerbread Day

(7th): National Chocolate Ice Cream Day

(8th): National Jelly-Filled Doughnut Day

(9th): National Strawberry-Rhubarb Pie Day

(10th): National Iced-Tea Day

(11th): National German Chocolate Cake Day

(12th): National Peanut Butter Cookie Day, International Falafel Day

(13th): Cupcake Lover's Day

(14th): National Strawberry Shortcake Day

(15th): Lobster Day

(16th): National Fudge Day

(17th): National Apple Strudel Day, National Cherry Tart Day

(18th): International Picnic Day, National Cheesemakers Day

(19th): National Martini Day

(20th): National Vanilla Milkshake Day

(21st): National Peaches & Cream Day

(22nd): National Chocolate Éclair Day, National Onion Ring Day

(23rd): National Pecan Sandy Day

(24th): National Pralines Day

(25th): National Strawberry Parfait Day, National Catfish Day

(26th): National Chocolate Pudding Day

(27th): National Orange Blossom Day

(28th): National Tapioca Day

(29th): National Almond Buttercrunch Day

(30th): National Mai Tai Day

# Section V:
# Meals for Every Craving –
# Beef, Chicken, Fish, & Pork

# History of Beef

*Beef* is the culinary name for meat from cattle, particularly skeletal muscle. Humans have been eating beef since prehistoric times. Beef is a source of high-quality nutrients.

Beef skeletal muscle meat can be used as is by merely cutting into certain parts, roast, short ribs, or steak (filet mignon, sirloin steak, rump steak, rib eye steak, hanger steak, etc.), while other cuts are processed (corned beef or beef jerky). Trimmings, on the other hand, are usually mixed with meat from older, leaner (therefore tougher) cattle, are ground, minced or used in sausages. The blood is used in some varieties called blood sausage. Other parts that are eaten include other muscles and offal, such as the oxtail, liver, tongue, tripe from the reticulum or rumen, glands (particularly the pancreas and thymus, referred to as sweetbread), the heart, the brain (although forbidden where there is a danger of bovine spongiform encephalopathy, BSE, commonly referred to as mad cow disease), the kidneys, and the tender testicles of the bull(known in the United States as calf fries, prairie oysters , or Rocky Mountain oysters). Some intestines are cooked and eaten as is but are more often cleaned and used as natural sausage casings. The bones are used for making beef stock.

Beef from steers and heifers is similar. Depending on economics, the number of heifers kept for breeding varies. The meat from older bulls, because it is usually tougher, is frequently used for mince (known as ground beef in the United States). Cattle raised for beef may be allowed to roam free on grasslands, or may be confined at some stage in pens as part of a large feeding operation called a feedlot (or concentrated animal feeding operation), where they are usually fed a ration of grain, protein, roughage and a vitamin/mineral pre-blend.

Beef is the third most widely consumed meat in the world, accounting for about 25% of meat production worldwide, after pork and poultry at 38% and 30%, respectively. In absolute numbers, the United States, Brazil, and the People's Republic of China are the world's three largest consumers of beef. Uruguay, however, has the highest beef and veal consumption per capita, followed by Argentina and Brazil. According to the data from OECD, the average Uruguayan ate over 42 Kg (93 lbs.) of beef or veal in 2014, representing the highest beef/veal consumption per capita in the world. In comparison, the average American consumed only about 24 Kg (53 lb.) beef or veal in the same year, while African countries, such as Mozambique, Ghana, and Nigeria, consumed the least beef or veal per capita.

Cows are considered sacred in the Hinduism and most observant Hindus who do eat meat almost always abstain from beef.

In 2015, the world's largest exporters of beef were India, Brazil, and Australia. Beef production is also important to the economies of Uruguay, Canada, Paraguay, Mexico, Argentina, Belarus and Nicaragua.

# History of Chicken

*Chicken*: Given the ubiquity of poultry on plates today, it may come as a surprise to learn domesticated chicken was not for eating but for fighting. Humans raised fowl for cockfights starting in Southeast Asia and China as early as 10,000 years ago, but their meat wasn't enjoyed until later. Now researchers investigating an ancient city in Israel have found what they think is the earliest evidence that chickens were kept for food.

For NPR, Dan Charles reports on the find from Maresha, a city that enjoyed its peak during 400 to 200 BC. There, archeologist including Lee Perry-Gal, a doctoral student in archeology at the University of Haifa, found more than a thousand chicken bones bearing the marks of the knives used to butcher them. Critically, they found twice as many female remains as male ones. The ladies don't fight, so all the signs point to chickens headed for dinner plates. Charles writes that something happened in Maresha to make the people think of chickens as food:

"Maybe, in the dry Mediterranean climate, people learned better how to raise large numbers of chickens in captivity. Maybe the chickens evolved, physically, and became more attractive as food."

But Perry-Gal thinks that part of it must have been a shift in the way people thought about food. "This is a matter of culture," she says. "You have to decide that you are eating chicken from now on."

The researchers published their findings in *Proceedings of the National Academy of Sciences*. They write that the earliest evidence of large-scale chicken eating in Europe only pops up during the first century B.C.E., at least 100 years later than the finds in Israel.

From the streets and houses of Maresha, the chicken's popularity started to boom. In recent years, the popularity of chicken on U.S. plates has finally surpassed that of beef. Now, Americans eat more than 80 pounds of chicken per person every year.

# History of Fish

*Fish*: The practice of fasting and abstaining from certain foods is an ancient one that has been practiced by many religions.

In the early years of Christianity in Europe, the Church instituted the practice of requiring the faithful to abstain from eating meat on Fridays in memory of Christ's death. During the season of Lent, the Church also called for abstaining from eating meat on Wednesdays as well as on Fridays.

While the Church called upon all of the adult faithful to abstain from meat on these days, the rule really only applied to the rich as the poor generally could not afford meat. As many vegetarians and environmentalists point out, producing meat is a more costly way of providing the nutrition humans need as it takes time for the animals to grow to maturity and, during this period of growth, they are consuming plant life.

Humans, being omnivorous, are able to consume and digest both plant and animal life, which means it is more efficient, from a production standpoint, to produce and eat the plant life directly rather than produce it to feed animals and then eating the animals.

It is important to note that the Church's directive called for abstaining from eating meat and did not mention, let alone require or even encourage, the eating of fish on Fridays.

The Church's objective in calling on the faithful to abstain from eating meat on certain days was to provide them with a simple exercise to aid in their spiritual development.

Human nature being what it is people usually react to new rules by looking for loopholes that enable them to comply with the letter of the rule but not necessarily the spirit of the rule.

In its abstinence rule, the Church simply required its members to abstain from eating meat, with the idea that people would limit their food to vegetables and grains on Fridays.

Meat is generally considered to be the flesh of warm-blooded land animals. Fish, on the other hand, are cold blooded water dwelling creatures. Using this technicality, people began consuming the flesh of fish in place of the flesh of animals on days of abstinence.

Fish thus became part of the culture of the Catholic Church.

People, of course, had been eating fish since the beginning of time, but the consumption of fish was limited to areas near waters where fish were plentiful.

St. Peter and some of the other Apostles and disciples of Jesus were fisherman. The New Testament describes Christ both accompanying them on a fishing trip and eating fish with them.

So, while the eating of fish had nothing to do with the fact that some of the Apostles were fisherman, the abstinence rule did begin the slow process of making fish more common among the Catholic population in general, and this slowly lead to some other economic and cultural changes in society.

As Europe emerged from the middle Ages and began growing economically, a middle class began to form. While lacking nobile titles and aristocratic ancestors, this group became the economic equals of the nobility and their rising incomes meant that the middle class could now afford to eat meat regularly as well.

This, of course made them consumers of fish as they now had to follow the abstinence rules of their faith. The Industrial Revolution caused the middle and working class to expand further as wages for factory workers began to rise. The economic growth produced by the Industrial Revolution attracted swarms of immigrants to North America.

Many of these immigrants came from Catholic countries in southern and eastern Europe, as well as numerous immigrants from heavily Catholic Ireland and Germany. As the incomes of these immigrants rose, they too found themselves able to afford more meat in their diets and, as a consequence found themselves substituting fish for meat on Fridays, just like the aristocratic lords in Medieval Europe, in order to comply with the rules of their faith.

Soon fish consumption by people living in America's interior cities like Louisville, Kentucky, Milwaukee, Wisconsin, St. Louis, Missouri, and others equaled that of areas along the Atlantic coast whose fishermen ended up supplying much of the cod and haddock sold in the interior. The increased consumption of fish in the industrial cities of the interior soon gave rise to the tradition of the Friday night Fish Fry, a custom that can still be found to this day in many of these cities.

With the advent of the five-day workweek, Friday became the end of the workweek as well as the anniversary of the day on which Our Lord was crucified. Soon restaurants began offering Friday fish fry as a relatively inexpensive way for working- and middle-class Catholics to dine out with their families while abiding by the precepts of their faith.

The restaurants were soon joined by local Catholic Churches, American Legion, and VFW Halls and other organizations, which found inexpensive fish fry dinners to be a good way for their members and others to get together and socialize while, at the same time, raising money for the churches or organizations. Things began to change following the Second Vatican Council, which met from October 11, 1962 to December 8, 1965. In early 1966 Pope Paul VI urged that the practice of fasting and abstinence be adapted to local economic conditions. Later that year the U.S. Conference of Catholic Bishops relaxed, but did not abolish, the rules on fasting and abstinence. However, the media and much of the laity interpreted these actions as abolishing the Church's requirement that the faithful abstain from meat on Fridays during the year and on Wednesdays and Fridays during Lent.

# History of Pork

*Pork* is the culinary name for meat from a domestic pig (Sus scrofa domesticus). It is the most commonly consumed meat worldwide, with evidence of pig husbandry dating back to 5000 BC. Pork is eaten both freshly cooked and preserved. Curing extends the shelf life of the pork products. Ham, smoked pork, gammon, bacon and sausage are examples of preserved pork. Charcuterie is the branch of cooking devoted to prepared meat products, many from pork.

Pork is the most popular meat in Eastern and Southeastern Asia, and is also very common in the Western world, especially in Central Europe. It is highly prized in Asian cuisines for its fat content and pleasant texture. Consumption of pork is forbidden by Jewish, Muslim, and Rastafarian dietary law, for religious reasons, with several suggested possible causes. The sale of pork is limited in Israel and illegal in certain Muslim countries.

# Acapulco Rice

Contributed by Isidro Teran

### Ingredients
1 eight-ounce bag jalapeno chips
2 three-ounce packages spam or Vienna sausage
1/2 of a nine-ounce dill pickle
2 jalapeno peppers (1.3-ounce singles)
1/2 of an eight-ounce bag of instant rice
1 two-ounce bag of salted peanuts
2 packets chicken seasoning from Ramen
2 twelve-ounce V-8 juices
4 tablespoons salsa
1 sixteen-ounce bag of tortilla chips

### Directions
You will need two hot pots and four large chip bags for this recipe.
Crush jalapeno chips; dice spam, pickle, and jalapeno peppers. Set
the salsa and the tortilla chips aside. Divide all remaining ingredients
equally in half. Place half in one chip bag and half in the other chip
bag. Mix well and tie off bags. Double bag each before placing in
each in a separate hot pot. Allow to cook for 3 hours. When cook
time is up, pour each bag in separate spread bowls. Top with the
salsa and break out the tortilla chips.

The measure of who we are is
what we do with what we have.
– Vince Lombardi.

# Bacon Deluxe Sandwich

Contributed by Scott Golden

### Ingredients
1 two-and-three-quarter-ounce bag of pork skins
2 three-ounce packages spam
2 tablespoons salad dressing
3·tablespoons hot water
4 slices bread
3 tablespoons squeeze cheese

### Directions
Leave pork skins whole and using hot water, hydrate in bag by lightly kneading until hydrated. Place 1 package of spam on a slice of bread and top with half the pork skins. Layer this with salad dressing and squeeze cheese. Top with other piece of bread. Grab your favorite chips and drink. You can add pickles and peppers if you desire the "Big Boy" Bacon Deluxe.

All great and honorable actions
are accompanied with great difficulties.
– William Bradford,
*History of Plymouth Plantation*

# BBQ Shack Sandwich

Contributed by Joseph Linden

## Ingredients

1/2 of a nine-ounce dill pickle
2 jalapeno peppers (1.3-ounce singles)
1/2 of an eight-ounce bag Shabang chips
1 eleven-and-a-quarter-ounce package of BBQ beef
1 packet of lemon lime electrolyte (.34-ounce)*
2 tablespoons onion flakes
1 packet beef seasoning from Ramen
4 tablespoons ketchup
6 slices bread

## Directions

Cut up pickle and jalapeno peppers into small pieces. Crush chips. Set aside ketchup and bread. Add remaining ingredients to the chip bag and knead. Place bag in a hot pot to heat for 2 hours. Stir occasionally. Remove bag from hot pot after cooked and spread 1/3 ketchup on a piece of bread. Top with BBQ mixture and another piece of bread. Should make 3 thick and delicious sandwiches. Welcome to the BBQ shack!

*Package of electrolyte is equal to 1 tablespoon electrolyte or 4 tablespoons Kool-Aid.

Courage in danger is half the battle.
– Plautus

# Boneless Hot Wings

Contributed by Dusty Rhodes

### Ingredients
1 seven-ounce package of chicken chunks
1/4 of an eight-ounce bottle of habanero sauce
1 packet of ranch dressing (1.5-ounce) *
1 eight-ounce bag of Shabang chips*
1 two-and-three-quarter-ounce bag of pork skins

### Directions
Drain and shred chicken chunks. Crush chips into a fine powder. Add chicken chunks to chip bag and knead these ingredients together. Begin to pour habanero sauce into the bag as you knead. You want to create a paste mixture. Not too wet – only moist enough to stick everything together. Once kneaded, divide mixture into 4-6 parts. Shape each part into an oval. Now crush pork skins into a super fine powder. Drop each part of chicken mixture into pork skins bag and shake to coat each one. Once all parts are coated, place 3 into a rice bag and place in a hot pot to cook for 3 hours. It is best to use two hot pots if you have access. Once all are done, place in a spread bowl and cover with ranch. Now that you have your main course you can go to sides section to complete your meal. Not quite like home, but probably as close as you can get.

*Shabang chips are somewhat close to salt & vinegar chips. Feel free to substitute.
*Packet of ranch dressing is equal to 2 tablespoons.

Never take counsel of your fears.
– Andrew Jackson

Troy Traylor

# Breaded Hot Dog Supreme

Contributed by Troy Traylor

**Ingredients**
1 two-and-a-three quarters-ounce bag of pork skins
1/2 of a nine-ounce pickle
4 tablespoons salad dressing
squeeze cheese to taste
2 jalapeno peppers (1.3-ounce singles)
4 hot dogs (cooked)
4 flour tortillas
condiments of choice (optional)

**Directions**
Perfect meal for an "Ad-Seg" offender (administrative segregation).
Crush pork skins into a fine powder. Cut up jalapeno peppers and
pickle. Lightly coat hot dogs with a little salad dressing. Drop hot
dogs into pork skins bag and shake to thoroughly coat. Now cover
the flour tortillas with squeeze cheese and the remaining salad
dressing. You can add some left-over pork skins as well if you
desire. Roll up tortillas and eat up!

The best and the most beautiful things in the
world cannot be seen or even touched,
they must be felt with the heart.
– Helen Keller.

# Chicken Cordon Bleu

Contributed by Christopher Camden

### Ingredients
1 three-ounce package of spam
1 seven-ounce package chicken chunks
2 jalapeno peppers (1.3-ounce singles)
1 packet of brown gravy mix (.75-ounce)
1 teaspoon garlic powder
salt and pepper to taste
4 tablespoons hot water
4 flour tortillas
4 tablespoons squeeze cheese

### Directions
Cut up spam into small strips and shred chicken chunks. Dice up the jalapeno peppers. In a small spread bowl combine spam and chicken chunks and knead into a pasty substance. Now in a cup or another small bowl, combine gravy mix and all seasonings with the hot water and mix until dissolved. Pour gravy into spam mixture and mix thoroughly. Spoon mixture onto four flour tortillas and roll up. Place tortillas in a rice bag and place the bag in a hot pot to heat for 2 hours. Once cook time is complete, place all four in a large spread bowl and top with squeeze cheese. White gravy also goes well with this meal if you prefer.

When you get into a tight place and it seems you
can't go on ... hold on for that's just the place
and the time when the tide will turn.
– Harriet Beecher Stowe

# Chicken Pot Pie

Contributed by Troy Traylor

**Ingredients**

1 seven-ounce package chicken chunks (shredded)
2 three-ounce chicken Ramen noodles
3 jalapeno peppers (1.3-ounce singles)
2 eight-ounce bags Shabang chips*
2½ coffee mugs hot water
1 ten-ounce bag flour tortillas
1/3 of a sixteen-ounce bottle squeeze cheese
habanera sauce, salsa, and black pepper to taste

**Directions**

Rinse off meat package and place in a hot pot to heat for 30 minutes. High-temperature hot pots work best. Crush up Ramen noodles. Dice jalapeno peppers and lightly crush all of the chips. Combine both bags of chips in one chip bag and add the Ramen noodles, jalapeno peppers, hot water, and black pepper. Knead the ingredients well. Wrap the bag in a towel and allow cooking for 10 minutes. All the water will absorb. Line a large spread bowl with four of the tortillas. Cover them with squeeze cheese and spoon on just half the Ramen mixture. Cover this mixture with shredded chicken chunks. Splash on your habanero sauce and top with remaining chip mixture. Add more squeeze cheese and four more flour tortillas. Press down firmly. Top with salsa or eat as is. Welcome to the freeworld!

*Shabang chips are not available everywhere so you can substitute with Salt & Vinegar.

> Tough times never last, tough people do.
> – Robert Schuller

# Chicken-Ramen Wraps

Contributed by Christopher Camden

**Ingredients**
2 seven-ounce packages chicken chunks
(or 2 nice size chicken quarters)
2 three-ounce chicken Ramen noodles
3 coffee mugs of hot water
2 tablespoons hot sauce
3 coffee mugs corn chips
1½ coffee mugs instant chili beans
1/4 of a sixteen-ounce bottle of squeeze cheese
1/2 of a fifteen-ounce bottle of sandwich spread
6 flour tortillas

**Directions**
Shred chicken chunks or chicken quarters. Crush Ramen soup and place both in a large spread bowl, with the seasoning packet. Add instant chili beans and hot water to bowl. Stir, and cover bowl tightly to heat for 10-12 minutes. Once cook time has expired, drain most of the remaining water, leaving the mixture a little wet. Now add the squeeze cheese, hot sauce, and sandwich spread to mixture and mix well. Now add the corn chips (lightly crushed, if you desire) to the bowl and mix again. Cover bowl for 15 minutes and allow chips to soften a bit. Roll mixture up in flour tortillas and enjoy your meal. This dish is best served cold.

(If you want to be a little creative with the recipe, add electrolyte or a couple of tablespoons of Kool Aid, it really enhances the flavor. Lemon or orange work best.)

The great remedy for anger is delay. – Seneca

# Christmas Dish

Contributed by Robby Hickox

**Ingredients**
2 three-ounce spicy vegetable Ramen
4 coffee mugs of hot water
1 nine-ounce dill pickle
1 three-ounce bag nacho chips
2 coffee mugs instant chili beans
1 five-ounce summer sausage
1/2 coffee mug black olives
5 tablespoons BBQ sauce
3 tablespoons salad dressing (or mayo)
3 tablespoons soy sauce
6-8 tablespoons of honey (to taste)
squeeze cheese to taste

**Directions**
Crush Ramen and place all in a large spread bowl. Add instant chili and hot water to bowl. Stir well while adding seasonings from Ramen. Cover bowl tightly and allow cooking for 10 minutes. While waiting, dice up summer sausage, pickle, and olives. Also crush chips. Once Ramen mixture is ready, set soy sauce aside and add all remaining ingredients to the bowl. Mix well and top with soy sauce. The reason this is a "Christmas dish" is because it is impossible to get olives unless it is Christmas. Happy Holidays!

The steps of faith fall on the seeming
void and find the rock beneath.
– John Greenleaf Whittier

# Creamy Beef Goulash

Contributed by Troy Traylor

### Ingredients
1 three-ounce package dehydrated mushrooms
1 three-ounce package dehydrated tomato/chilies
10 tablespoons instant milk
3½ coffee mugs hot water
1 eleven-and-a-quarter-ounce package BBQ beef
1 package beef seasoning from Ramen
1 one-and-three-quarter-ounce bottle onion flakes
1 three-quarter-ounce package brown gravy
3 three-ounce beef Ramen noodles
1 three-ounce bag regular potato chips

### Directions
Use a large chip bag, 16-ounce, and combine the dehydrated
ingredients, instant milk and 1½ coffee mugs of hot water. Stir until
everything is dissolved. Now add the BBQ beef, 1 seasoning packet
from Ramen, onion flakes, and brown gravy mix. Again, stir until
everything is dissolved. Double bag and place in a hot pot to heat for
2 hours. Stir occasionally. While this is cooking, lightly crush Ramen
in a large spread bowl. Add two coffee mugs hot water to Ramen,
cover tightly, and let cook for just 3 minutes. Drain off any excess
water from Ramen. Once cooked, remove beef mixture from hot pot
and pour into Ramen noodles. Stir well then cover tightly and let
cook for an additional 3 minutes. Top with crushed chips. If you can
get buttered bread, you're in for a truly delicious meal. Sooo good.

> Too soon old; Too late smart.
> – Amish Saying

# Delicious Chicken and Dumplings

Contributed by Kendall Hartl-Cantu

## Ingredients

1 seven-ounce package chicken chunks
2 three-ounce chicken Ramen noodles
2 coffee mugs hot water
1 sleeve snack crackers
1 package Cheese & Chive crackers
(1.375-ounces)
3 tablespoons BBQ sauce
3 tablespoons squeeze cheese

## Directions

Rinse off meat package and place in a hot pot to heat. (Two hot pots would be a big help with this recipe. Find the hottest pots you have access to.) Lightly crush Ramen and place all in a large spread bowl. Add 1¾ coffee mugs hot water to the bowl and cover tightly. Allow this to cook for 10 minutes. While cooking, crush snack and Cheese & Chive crackers. Combine these ingredients in a separate spread bowl and mix. Carefully add approximately 2 tablespoons of hot water as you knead into dough. Once you have a "doughy" consistency, divide into parts and roll each one into dime-size balls. These are your dumplings. Once Ramen is ready, combine all ingredients in a large spread bowl and mix well. If there is water left in Ramen, do not drain.

> Life with Fools consist in Drinking;
> With the wise Man, living's Thinking.
> – Benjamin Franklin, *Poor Richard's Almanack*

# Dream's Chino Bowl

Contributed by Dusty Rhodes

**Ingredients**
1 eight-ounce bag instant rice
6 packets of orange electrolyte (.34-ounce each)*
7 coffee mugs hot water
1/4 of a fifteen-ounce bag refried beans
1 one-ounce fruit stick
2 three-ounce chili Ramen noodles
3 jalapeno peppers(1.3-ounce singles)
1 nine-ounce pickle
2 three-and-a-half-ounce packages of mackerel
1/4-1/3 of a twelve-ounce jar of grape jelly (to taste)
1 two-and-three-quarter-ounce bag of pork skins
1/2 of an eight-ounce bag of Shabang chips
1/4 of a sixteen-ounce bag corn chips
squeeze cheese and BBQ sauce to taste
chili garlic/habanera (optional) to taste

**Directions**
This recipe takes some work, but it is worth it. You will need 3 large
spread bowls. In bowl 1, combine rice, electrolytes, and 3 coffee
mugs of hot water. Stir well, cover tightly, and let cook for 10-12
minutes. In bowl 2, combine refried beans with 1½ coffee mugs hot
water. Cover this bowl tightly and let cook 10-12 minutes. Now crush
up fruit stick and Ramen noodles. Combine these in bowl 3, with 2
coffee mugs of hot water. Stir and cover tightly for 5-8 minutes.
While these bowls cook, cut up jalapeno peppers and pickle. Drain
mackerels. Add 4 tablespoons of hot water to jelly and break it
down. Once jelly is broken down, pour it into pork skins bag and

lightly knead until the skins are hydrated thoroughly. Set this to the side for a moment. When the bowls are ready, drain any excess water from each. It is probably best to use two bowls and equally divide these three bowls. Mix each bowl well. Divide the mackerel, jalapeno peppers, and pickles between these two bowls and mix thoroughly. Wash out the third bowl and line the bottom and sides of it with Shabang chips. Spoon the rice mixture into this bowl. Crush the corn chips and pour half on top of the rice mixture. Cover with cheese and BBQ sauce. If you opt to use chili garlic, add it now. Finally, it is time to top-off your bowl with half of your pork skins. Repeat this with the remaining ingredients. Now that you have worked up an appetite, invite an associate to join you for a grand meal.

*Packages of electrolytes are equal to 1 tablespoon electrolyte or 4 tablespoons of Kool-Aid each.

The man who strives to educate himself – and no one else can educate him – must win a certain victory over his own nature. He must learn to smile at his dear idols, analyze his every prejudice, scrap if necessary, his fondest and most consoling belief, question his presuppositions, and take his chances with the truth.
– Everett Dean Martin

# Dreamy Rice

Contributed by Daniel Cortez

### Ingredients
1 eight-ounce bag jalapeno chips
1 two-and-three-quarter-ounce bag pork skins
1 five-ounce summer sausage
1 package beef seasoning from Ramen
1/2 of an eight-ounce bag instant rice
1 twelve-ounce V-8 juice
1/2 coffee mug of hot water

### Directions
Crush chips, dice summer sausage, and lightly crush pork skins. Combine all the ingredients in the jalapeno chip bag, double bag them, and place in a hot pot to heat for 2-3 hours, stirring occasionally. After cooking is complete, pour all into a large spread bowl and mix well, then "dig in"! MMM good!

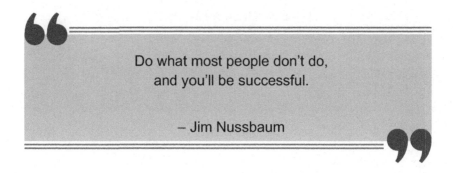

Do what most people don't do,
and you'll be successful.

– Jim Nussbaum

Troy Traylor

# Egg Ramen Breakfast

Contributed by James Campbell Jr.

### Ingredients
1 three-ounce Ramen noodles (seasoning package not needed)
1½ coffee mugs hot water
4 hard-boiled eggs
1¼ tablespoons soy sauce*

### Directions
Crush Ramen noodles and place in a large
spread bowl with hot water. Cover tightly
and cook for 10 minutes. While you wait, peel and
dice eggs. After cooking, drain any excess water from Ramen and
add the eggs and soy sauce. Mix well.

*If you do not have soy sauce, in a coffee cup combine 1/4
tablespoon of cheap coffee, 1 seasoning package of beef seasoning
from Ramen noodles, and 1/4 of a coffee mug of hot water. Stir until
all is dissolved.

> The ability to keep a cool head in an emergency,
> maintain poise in the midst of excitement,
> and refuse to be stampeded are true marks of leadership.
> – R. Shannon

# Fabulous Fishy Burgers

Contributed by Don Meyers

## Ingredients
2 three-ounce Ramen noodles
1 two-and-three-quarter-ounce bag of pork skins
1/4 of an eight-ounce bag of jalapeno chips
2 jalapeno peppers (1.3 ounce singles)
2 four-and-a-quarter-ounce packages of tuna
2¼ coffee mugs of hot water
1/3 of a sixteen-ounce bottle squeeze cheese
4 heaping tablespoons sandwich spread
8 slices bread

## Directions
Crush the Ramen, pork skins, and jalapeno chips. Combine all in a large chip bag. Drain the tuna and dice the jalapeno peppers and add both to the bag. Pour in the hot water and knead thoroughly, until most of the water is absorbed. Flatten out in the bag like a pizza, even out, and wrap in some newspaper or a towel. Set this aside to cook for 15-minutes. Once cooked cut bag open long-ways, and using your ID card, cut the mixture the size of bread slices. Place one square on a slice of bread and top with cheese and sandwich spread and then another slice of bread. There you have it. Makes 4 Fabulous Fishy Burgers. Enjoy with chips and a cold drink.

Bigness comes from doing many small things well.
Individually, they are not very dramatic transactions.
Together, though, they may add up.
– Edward S. Finkelstein

# Fishy Rice

Contributed by Chad Ritchie

### Ingredients
1 eight-ounce bag of instant rice
3 coffee mugs hot water
12-15 packets of mayonnaise (approximately 5 heaping tablespoons)
1 bag sliced jalapeno peppers (.7 ounces)
6 flour tortillas
2 packages of butter (approximately 5-6 tablespoons)
1 ten-ounce bag black beans (about 1¾ coffee mugs)
4 three-and-a-half-ounce packs of fish (preferably in spicy mustard)
1 nine-ounce hot pickle (optional)
habanera sauce to taste

### Directions
Combine rice and hot water in a large bowl. Cover tightly to cook for 10 minutes. Afterward, add mayo and mix well. Leave the bowl uncovered to completely cool (use ice to accelerate cooling, if you have access). Finely dice the pickle and jalapeno pepper and set aside. Use a spork (a cross between a spoon and a fork) to poke holes in the flour tortillas and cover each one with butter. Line a microwave with paper towels (to reduce mess) and heat tortillas for 45-60 seconds. Flip and repeat. You want your tortilla shells crisp and light brown. When rice has cooled, rinse the black beans, add them, the packages of fish (drain if in oil), and the jalapeno pepper pieces and pickle mix well. Separate this mixture into two bowls and top both with habanera sauce to taste. Now either top each bowl with crushed up tortilla shells or place the mixture on the shells and eat tostada style.

> When anger arises think of the consequences.
> – Confucius

# Game Day Appetizer

Contributed by Robert Henderson

## Ingredients
1 eight-ounce package Mexican beef crumbles
1 package chili seasoning from Ramen
8 jalapeno peppers(1.3 ounce singles)
1/3 of a sixteen-ounce bottle of squeeze cheese
1/2 of a sixteen-ounce bag of corn chips
1 twelve-ounce V-8 juice
3 two-ounce packages cream cheese*
1/4 jar of salsa

## Directions
Crumble Mexican beef crumbles until fine. Crush corn chips until fine. Combine in a large spread bowl. Add the chili seasoning and enough V-8 to make a moist dough (a little less than a quarter of the can, approximately). Knead this into a dough and then roll it out on top of plastic or a chip bag. Now cut jalapeno peppers in half, length wise, and clean out insides and seeds. Now use a hot pot lid and cut dough into circles. Fill each jalapeno half with cream cheese and then roll up in a dough circle and pinch closed. Shape into an egg shape. Put 3-4 each in separate rice bags. Place bag in a hot pot to heat for 1 hour (try to find the hottest pot you have access to). After cooking, place eggs in a spread bowl and top with squeeze cheese and salsa. These appetizers will have you looking forward to each game day.

*Packages of cream cheese are equal to 4 tablespoons each.

> Light is the task where many share the toil.
> – Homer

# Ham-Burgers

Contributed by Troy Traylor

## Ingredients

1 eleven-and-a-quarter-ounce package chili no beans
1 eight-ounce bag BBQ chips
8 slices white bread
2 tablespoons squeeze cheese
1 sleeve snack crackers
1 nine-ounce dill pickle (any flavor)
4 three-ounce packages spam
4 tablespoons salad dressing
salt and black pepper to taste

## Directions

Rinse off meat package and place in a hot pot to heat for 30 minutes (or until hot). While waiting crush up the crackers and chips and dice the pickle. After cooking the chili, combine with the snack crackers, and chips in the chip bag and knead thoroughly. Flatten out the mixture in the chip bag, even out the thickness, and form into a pizza shape. Wrap in newspaper or a towel and set aside for 15 minutes. After this has set up, cut open the bag length wise and use your ID to cut the mixture into squares the size of bread. Place 1 square on each of 4 pieces of bread and top with 1 package of spam each. Now add the pickle, salt, pepper, cheese, salad dressing, and another square of mixture. Now cap off with another slice of bread. You now have 4 Big Boy Ham-Burgers. Call your closest associate. What a treat with a cold drink and your favorite chips.

> It's never too late to be what you might have been.
> – George Eliot

# Homemade Hot Pocket

Contributed by Benito Gutierrez

**Ingredients**
3 coffee mugs whole wheat cereal
4 slices sweet ham
3 hard-boiled eggs
4 tablespoons squeeze cheese
1 loaf white bread
4 slices turkey
4 slices salami
1 Tijuana Mama pickled sausage
1/4 eight-ounce bag BBQ chips
1/4 coffee mug hot water

**Directions**
Crush the cereal in a large spread bowl and combine it with the bread and enough water to make a dough-like substance – just wet enough for it all to stick together. Once formed, roll dough out on a piece of plastic to about an inch in thickness in a square shape. Cut in half and allow to setup for 1 hour. While waiting, cut up the meats and eggs. Also crush chips fairly fine. Once drying time has expired, divide remaining ingredients in half and place on one side of each piece of dough. Fold each over and pinch all around edges so it closes up. Place one hot pocket each in a separate rice bag and place each in a separate hot pot to cook for 2 hours. Once done, remove from hot pot and coat with squeeze cheese. Sprinkle chips over top of this.

There is more to life than books. But not much more.
– Morrissey

# Hot & Spicy Chicken Wraps

Contributed by Carlos Espinoza

### Ingredients
2 seven-ounce packages chicken chunks
1/2 eight-ounce bottle habanero sauce
1/2 eight-ounce bag jalapeno chips
2 two-ounce packages cream cheese*
8 flour tortillas
2-3 tablespoons squeeze cheese
2 one-and-a-half-ounce packages ranch dressing*

### Directions
Shred chicken chunks and place all in a large spread bowl. Add habanero to this bowl and mix to coat all chicken. Cover bowl and marinade for 3 hours. Stir occasionally. Crush up chips while you wait. Once marinade time is up, add chips to bowl and mix thoroughly. Allow juice in bowl to be absorbed by chips. Spread some cream cheese on each flour tortilla and spoon chip mixture onto them. Roll these into your wraps and place 4 in a rice bag. Place bag in a hot pot to heat for 3-4 hours. Two pots work best or just repeat the steps. When these are done, place 4 in a large spread bowl and top with squeeze cheese and ranch dressing.

*Packages of cream cheese are equal to 4 tablespoons each.
*Packages of ranch dressing are equal to 2 tablespoons each.

> Knowledge has to be improved, challenged and increased constantly or it vanishes.
> – Peter Drucker

# Hot & Spicy Tuna Spread

Contributed by Troy Traylor

### Ingredients
1 eight-ounce bag instant rice
2½ coffee mugs hot water
2 jalapeno peppers (1.3-ounce singles)
2 four-and-a-quarter-ounce packages tuna
1 teaspoon garlic (heavy)
1 tablespoon onion powder
1 one-and-three-quarters-ounce bottle onion flakes
3/4 of a fifteen-ounce bottle sandwich spread
1/3 of a sixteen-ounce bottle squeeze cheese
1/4 of an eight-ounce bag BBQ chips
1 ten-ounce package flour tortillas
black pepper to taste

### Directions
In a large spread bowl, or in rice bag, combine rice and hot water. If you use a spread bowl, cover tightly and cook for 12-15 minutes. If you use the rice bag, seal bag, wrap in a towel, and allow cooking 10-12 minutes. I honestly prefer the rice bag. While waiting, cut up jalapeno peppers and drain tuna. Once rice is cooked, set chips and flour tortillas aside and combine the remaining ingredients. Mix thoroughly. Crush up chips. Spoon mixture onto flour tortillas and top with chips. Now roll them up. You can heat this a little if you want, but it is plenty good the way it is.

A small leak will sink a great ship.
– Benjamin Franklin

# Jambalaya

Contributed by Tom Orton

**Ingredients**

1 three-ounce Cajun chicken Ramen
1 eight-point-eight-ounce microwavable Jambalaya
8 coffee mugs hot water
2 five-ounce summer sausages
2 jalapeno peppers (1.3-ounce singles)
1 twelve-ounce bag instant chili beans*
1 ten-ounce bag black beans*

**Directions**

There are a few steps in preparing this meal and a microwave is
needed. Crush Ramen and leave in the bag. Add the seasoning to
bag and shake to coat all noodles. Cook the Jambalaya according to
directions. Add enough hot water to Ramen bag to cover noodles.
Use a pen to hold package closed. While all is cooking, dice the
jalapeno peppers. In a large spread bowl combine the summer
sausage, jalapeno peppers, instant chili beans, and black beans,
with remaining hot water. Stir well and cover bowl tightly. Allow this
to cook for 12-15 minutes. Once cook time is up, drain any excess
water. Add the Ramen and Jambalaya to bowl and mix thoroughly.

*Instant chili will be equal to 2 coffee mugs.
*Bag of black beans will be equal to 1¾ coffee mugs.

Discouragement and failure are two of the surest
stepping stones to success. – Dale Carnegie

# Legendary Chicken Pasta

Contributed by Troy Traylor

**Ingredients**
1 seven-ounce package chicken chunks
3 two-ounce packages cream cheese*
1½ teaspoons garlic powder
1 coffee mug crushed cheese puffs
1 twelve-ounce V-8 juice
5 tablespoons squeeze cheese
2 three-ounce chicken Ramen noodles

**Directions**
Shred chicken chunks and place in a large 16-ounce chip bag. Now add the V-8 juice, 2 packages cream cheese, squeeze cheese, garlic and 1 seasoning package from Ramen. Mix well, double bag, and place in a hot pot to heat for 1½ hours. While this cook, separate the Ramen in half, like bread. Break the halves into 4 pieces each. Place these in a large spread bowl. Crush the cheese puffs. Once chicken chunk mixture is hot, pour it into the Ramen bowl, stir, and cover tightly. Allow this to cook for 8 minutes, then stir, and add the remaining cream cheese and the cheese puffs. Stir well and dig in. (Save the other seasoning package for another recipe.)

*Packages of cream cheese are equal to 4 tablespoons each

> Many of our fears are tissue paper thin, and a single courageous step would carry us clear through them.
> – Brendan Francis

# Lemon Pepper Fish & Rice

Contributed by Troy Traylor

**Ingredients**

1 nine-ounce dill pickle
2 jalapeno peppers (1.3-ounce singles)
2 three-and-a-half-ounce packages mackerel
1 four-and-a-quarter-ounce package tuna with jalapenos
1 three-and-a-half-ounce package sardines (regular or hot)
1 eight-ounce bag instant rice
2½ coffee mugs hot water
2½ packets lemon lime electrolyte (.34 ounce)
3/4 of a fifteen-ounce bottle salad dressing
2 tablespoons black pepper
1 ten-ounce bag flour tortillas

**Directions**

Cut up pickle and jalapeno peppers and put in a large spread bowl, with the pickle juice. Drain all 3 meats and add them to this bowl. Break up and mix well. Cover bowl and allow all to marinade for 1 hour. After marinating, add the hot water to rice bag and wrap bag in a towel. Set aside for 10-12 minutes to cook. Once rice is ready, drain any water. Drain most of the juice from bowl of meat mixture. Add rice to bowl and mix very well. Now add the electrolytes, salad dressing, and black pepper. Mix again very thoroughly so electrolyte coats everything. Allow to cool to room temperature. Spoon on flour tortillas and roll or fold. This is an extremely good, cold dish. (Can also make the same way using orange electrolytes.)

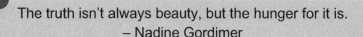

The truth isn't always beauty, but the hunger for it is.
– Nadine Gordimer

# Mac Daddy

Contributed by Troy Traylor

## Ingredients

1 eleven-and-a-quarter-ounce package chili with beans
4 three-and-a-half-ounce packages mackerel
1 nine-ounce pickle
3 jalapeno peppers(1.3-ounce singles)
1 eight-ounce bag instant rice
2 three-ounce chili Ramen noodles
4 coffee mugs hot water
3 tablespoons pickle juice
1 chili Ramen seasoning
1½ tablespoons garlic powder
1 light tablespoon onion powder
1/2 tablespoon black pepper
6 tablespoons sandwich spread
1/3 sixteen-ounce bottle squeeze cheese
1/3 sixteen-ounce corn chips
2 sleeves snack crackers or saltines

## Directions

Two hot pots work best for this recipe. You will also need two large spread bowls as well. Rinse off chili package and place in a hot pot to heat. Hotter the pot, the better. While waiting, drain juices from all mackerel, cut up pickle, and cut up jalapeno peppers. Add 1/2 the hot water to the rice bag (water should be about 2 inches above the rice) and wrap in a towel. Cook in bag for 15 minutes. Crush Ramen in their bags and remove seasoning packages. Add both Ramen to a large spread bowl and add the rest of the hot water. Cover bowl tightly and cook for 5-8 minutes. When rice and Ramen are cooked, drain any excess water from both. Put half the rice and 1 Ramen in each spread bowl and mix. Set corn chips aside for a moment. Now divide all the remaining ingredients in half and put half in one bowl and half in the other. Mix both very well. Now crush the corn chips and divide them between these two bowls. Mix again lightly. Hope you're hungry. Invite an associate to enjoy this one. Eat as it is or on snack crackers or saltines.

Rarely is it advisable to meet prejudices and passions
head on. Instead, it is best to appear to conform
to them in order to gain time to combat them.
One must know how to sail with a contrary wind
and tack until one meets a wind in the right direction.
– Fortune De Felice

# Man-wich

Contributed by Troy Traylor

## Ingredients
1 three-ounce chicken Ramen noodles
1½ coffee mugs hot water
1 three-ounce spam or favorite lunch meat
1 jalapeno pepper (1.3-ounce single)
1/4 of a nine-ounce dill pickle (any flavor)
2 slices white bread
mustard or salad dressing to taste

## Directions
Carefully separate Ramen in half without breaking apart. Place both halves in a spread bowl with the hot water. Cover tightly to cook for 5 minutes. Drain all water. Dice the jalapeno pepper and pickle. Now take one half of the Ramen and place it on a slice of bread. Top with meat, jalapeno pepper, and pickle. Sandwich with other half of Ramen. Sprinkle seasoning package over this and top with your mustard or salad dressing. Place other piece of bread on top and grab your favorite chips. Very simple and very good.

Once you choose hope, anything is possible.
- Christopher Reeve

# Not Quite Fried Rice

Contributed by Bob Leach

**Ingredients**

2½ coffee mugs hot water
2 three-and-a-half-ounce packages mackerel
1 pinch salt
1 eight-ounce bag instant rice
1 jalapeno pepper (1.3-ounce single)
1 tablespoon chili garlic sauce
1 two-ounce bag salted peanuts

**Directions**

Combine rice and hot water in a large spread bowl, cover tightly and cook for 15 minutes. While waiting, cut up jalapeno pepper and drain mackerel. Once rice is cooked, combine rice, pepper pieces, mackerel, chili garlic sauce, and salt in the spread bowl and mix well. Crush peanuts and add to bowl. Not quite fried rice, but one to talk about.

When one door closes, another opens; but we often look so long and so regretfully upon the closed door that we do not see the one that has opened for us.
– Alexander Graham Bell

# Nubs' Hot Pocket

Contributed by William Rowland

### Ingredients
1 sleeve saltine crackers
1½ coffee mugs crushed Cheese Puffs
3-4 tablespoons hot water
1 solid meat package of choice
1 jalapeno pepper (1.3-ounce single)
2 tablespoons squeeze cheese
1/2 of a two-ounce package of cream cheese

### Directions
Crush saltine crackers and Cheese Puffs into a fine powder and place in a large spread bowl. Pour 2 tablespoons hot water into this bowl and knead into a dough-like substance, adjusting consistency with a few more drops of water as you go. You do not want the dough wet. Flatten the dough in the bottom of the spread bowl and let dry for 30 minutes. While waiting, shred up or dice the meat of choice and cut up jalapeno pepper. When dough is ready, coat half with cheese and meat from package. Add your jalapeno pepper pieces and cream cheese to this. Now you want to flip other half over and pinch closed around the edges. Place this in a rice bag and set in a hot pot to heat for 1 hour. The hotter the pot, the better. If you use a chip bag to heat, be sure to double bag.

* Package of cream cheese is equal to 4 tablespoons. This recipe will feed two.

The first step is you have to say you can. – Will Smith.

# Nubs' Stuffed Baked Potato

Contributed by William Rowland

**Ingredients**

1 five-ounce summer sausage or 1 eleven-and-a-quarter-ounce package BBQ beef
1 eight-ounce bag jalapeno chips
1 eight-ounce bag BBQ chips
1 tablespoon butter if available
1 two-ounce package cream cheese
1 jalapeno pepper (1.3-ounce single)
1/3 coffee mug hot water
salt to taste

**Directions**

For summer sausage dice and put in a rice bag with 4 tablespoons hot water and heat in a hot pot for 1 hour. For BBQ beef, rinse package and heat in a hot pot for 1 hour. Crush both bags of chips and combine in 1 bag. Add a little hot water at a time while you knead. You only want it moist enough, so the chips soften and stick together. Flatten out mixture in bag once kneaded. Cut bag open length wise and let dry while meat is heating. Once meat is hot, place it on top of chip mixture. Cover just half the chip mixture and leave about 1½ inches from the edge. Flip other half over the top and pinch closed around the edges. Shape into a potato and place in a large chip bag, double bag, and place in a hot pot to heat for 1 hour. After cooking, sprinkle potato with salt and pepper and top with cream cheese. Now dice up jalapeno pepper and decorate. A freeworld taste for sure.

*Package of cream cheese is equal to 4 tablespoons.

> Regrets are as personal as fingerprints.
> – Margaret Culkin Banning

# Pizza Wraps

Contributed by Troy Traylor

## Ingredients
1/2 of a twenty-ounce bottle ketchup
1 tablespoon onion powder
1 tablespoon hot sauce
1 two-and-three-quarter-ounce bag pork skins
6 tablespoons squeeze cheese
1 heaping teaspoon garlic powder
2 tablespoons onion flakes
2 jalapeno peppers (1.3-ounce singles)
6·flour tortillas
1 three-and-a-half-ounce package pepperoni slices

## Directions
Combine ketchup, all seasonings, and hot sauce in a cup and mix well. This will be your sauce. Cut up jalapeno peppers and crush pork skins. Now coat the flour tortillas with squeeze cheese and top with pork skins and jalapenos. Add sauce to these and top with pepperoni. Roll up the tortillas and place all 6 in a rice bag. Place this bag in a hot pot to heat for 2 hours. Once all is ready, place these in a large spread bowl. If you have any sauce left over pour over pizza wraps. I hope you enjoy this one.

> If you wish success in life, make perseverance your bosom friend, experience your wise counselor, caution your elder brother, and hope your guardian genius. -- Joseph Addison

# Pour Étouffée over Bed of Rice

Contributed by Blair Blanchotto

### Ingredients
2 medium to large bell peppers
2 medium onions
4-6 sticks butter
2 ten-ounce cans cream of celery soup
2 ten-ounce cans cream of mushroom soup
6 coffee mugs instant rice
7 coffee mugs hot water
1/2 pound crawfish
1 tablespoon onion powder
1 tablespoon Lowry Season Salt

### Directions
Dice bell peppers and onion in a large pot, bring butter to a simmer over medium heat. Add bell peppers and onions to pot and cook for ten minutes. Add all cans of soup to pot and simmer while you cook rice separately. Once rice is cooked, drain excess water and add rice and crawfish to pot. Increase heat to high until it reaches the boiling point and then reduce to low heat. Cover pot and cook for 10 minutes. Turn off heat and add both seasonings. Stir well, then cover pot again and let sit for 5 more minutes.

Only those that dare to fail greatly can achieve greatly.
— Robert F. Kennedy

# Prison Style Thai Meal

Contributed by Tom Orton

### Ingredients
1 three-ounce beef Ramen noodles
2 coffee mugs hot water
1 tablespoon hot sauce
3 tablespoons butter
1 coffee mug carrots
2 tablespoons peanut butter
1 three-ounce chili Ramen noodles
2 jalapeno peppers (1.3-ounce singles)
4 tablespoons ketchup
4 tablespoons onion flakes
1 coffee mug peas
2-3 tablespoons soy sauce

### Directions
Crush both Ramen noodles and place in a spread bowl with seasoning packages. Add the hot water to bowl, stir, and cover tightly for 5 minutes. While waiting, dice up jalapeno peppers. Once Ramen is ready do not drain water. Set soy sauce aside and combine all remaining ingredients. If you have a microwave heat on medium heat until good and hot. If no microwave, place all in a large chip bag and double bag. Set down in a hot pot to heat for about 1 hour, or until good and hot. Once meal is hot, pour your soy sauce over top and give thanks for what you are about to receive.

Impatience never commanded success.
– Edwin H. Chapin

# Purple Haze Rice

Contributed by Uriel Rodriguez

### Ingredients

1 five-ounce summer sausage
1 eight-ounce bag instant rice
2 packets grape Kool-Aid* (.14-ounce)
2½ coffee mugs hot water
2 jalapeno peppers (1.3-ounce singles)
4 tablespoons mustard
1 two-and-three-quarter-ounce bag pork skins

### Directions

Dice summer sausage into tiny pieces and put in a rice bag.
Place rice bag in a hot pot to heat for 1 hour. About 15 minutes
before cooking is complete, combine rice, Kool Aid, and hot
water in a large spread bowl and mix well. Cover bowl tightly
and let cook for 15 minutes. Dice up jalapeno peppers while you
wait. Once cooked, combine summer sausage, rice, jalapeno
pepper pieces, and mustard in the spread bowl and mix well.
Lightly crush pork skins and add to bowl. Mix again. Now it's
time to dig in. This is one to try for sure. Has an amazing taste.

*Packages of Kool-Aid are equal to 2 tablespoons each.

We do not have to become heroes overnight. Just a step
at a time, meeting each thing that comes up …
discovering we have the strength to stare it down.
– Eleanor Roosevelt

# Ramen for One

Contributed by Troy Traylor

### Ingredients
1 three-ounce Ramen noodles (any flavor)
1 three-and-a-half-ounce package mackerel
1/4 of a nine-ounce dill pickle
1 good handful corn chips
1 coffee mug hot water
1 jalapeno pepper (1.3-ounce single)
3 tablespoons salad dressing

### Directions
Crush Ramen and place in a large spread bowl with seasoning. Add hot water to bowl, cover tightly, and let cook for 5 minutes. While waiting, drain mackerel, dice jalapeno pepper, and pickle. Once cook time is compete, drain excess water and combine all remaining ingredients. Mix well. This is as simple as it gets.

The most common way people give up their power is by thinking they don't have any
– Alice Walker,
Pulitzer Prize for Fiction recipient

# Ramen Noodle Salad

Contributed by John Black

### Ingredients
2 three-ounce packages spam
1 four-and-a-quarter-ounce package of tuna
1 three-ounce Ramen noodles (no seasoning)
1¼ coffee mug hot water
1 packet orange electrolyte* (.34-ounce)
1 two-ounce package cream cheese*
2 one-and-a-half-ounce packages ranch dressing*
3 tablespoons salsa

### Directions
Dice up the spam and drain tuna package. Crush Ramen. Combine Ramen with hot water and electrolyte in a large spread bowl, stir well, and cover tightly. Cook for 8 minutes. Now combine all remaining ingredients and stir until thoroughly mixed. Grab your spoon and dig in!

*Packet of electrolyte is equal to 1 tablespoon electrolyte or 4 tablespoons Kool-Aid.
*Package of cream cheese is equal to 4 tablespoons.
*Package of ranch dressing is equal to 2 tablespoons.

Time is really the only capital that any human being has, and the one thing that he can't afford to lose.
–Thomas A. Edison (1847-1931)

# Ramen Salad

Contributed by Troy Traylor

**Ingredients**
1 three-ounce chicken Ramen noodles
1 seven-ounce package chicken chunks
3/4 coffee mug hot water
1 coffee mug crushed party mix
1/2 nine-ounce dill pickle
1 two-ounce package trail mix
1½ tablespoons salad dressing
1 packet sweetener*

**Directions**
Crush Ramen and shred chicken chunks. Combine both ingredients with the hot water in a large spread bowl. Cover tightly and let cook for 10 minutes. While waiting crush the party mix and dice pickle. When cook time is complete, drain any excess water and combine remaining ingredients. Mix all well. A quick and easy meal.

*Packet of sweetener is equal to 2 teaspoons sugar

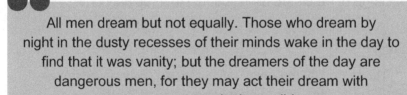

All men dream but not equally. Those who dream by night in the dusty recesses of their minds wake in the day to find that it was vanity; but the dreamers of the day are dangerous men, for they may act their dream with open eyes to make it possible.
– T.E. Lawrence

# Rockin Ranch Style Noodles

Contributed by Bob Leach

### Ingredients
1 three-ounce chicken Ramen noodles
3/4 coffee mug hot water
3 tablespoons butter
1 teaspoon garlic powder
1 teaspoon black pepper
1 sleeve snack crackers

### Directions
Slightly crush Ramen noodles and combine with seasoning package and hot water in a large spread bowl. Cover tightly and let cook 8-10 minutes. Drain any excess water and stir in butter, garlic, and black pepper. Mix well. That's it! Eat on snack crackers. That's how we do it Rockin Ranch Style.

Be more concerned about your character than your reputation, because your character is what you really are, while your reputation is merely what others think you are.
– John Wooden, Basketball coach of UCLA

# Savory Tuna Melts

Contributed by Carlos Espinoza

Ingredients
2 four-and-a-quarter-ounce packages tuna
1/2 eight-ounce bag jalapeno chips
4 two-ounce packages cream cheese*
6 flour tortillas
2 jalapeno peppers(1.3-ounce singles)
5 tablespoons squeeze cheese
1 package chili seasoning from Ramen
2 one-and-a-half-ounce packages ranch or light salsa*

**Directions**
This is a recipe that will leave you wanting more. Drain tuna, dice jalapeno peppers, and crush up chips. In a large spread bowl, combine these three ingredients and add the squeeze cheese and cream cheese to bowl as well. Mix all well. Now sprinkle in chili seasoning and roll all up in the flour tortillas. Place all in your spread bowl and top with your choice of ranch dressing or light salsa. Truly a mouth-watering dish.

*Packages of cream cheese are equal to 4 tablespoons each.
*Packages of ranch dressing are equal to 2 tablespoons each.

> You had better live your best and act your best and think your best today: for today is the sure preparation for tomorrow and all the other tomorrows that follow.
> – Harriet Martineau

# Smoked Tomato Sandwich

Contributed by Troy Traylor

**Ingredients**
1 eight-ounce bag BBQ chips
4 tablespoons salad dressing
1/2 coffee mug ketchup
8 slices white bread
salt and black pepper to taste

**Directions**
Crush chips into a fine powder and place all in a large spread bowl. Add ketchup to bowl and mix to coat chips. Allow to sit 5 minutes so all softens and absorbs. Add in salt and pepper and mix again. Coat your bread with the salad dressing and top with chip mixture. Now cover with another slice of bread and enjoy the flavor.

Great beauty, great strength, and great riches are really and truly of no greater use; a right heart exceeds all.
– Benjamin Franklin, *Poor Richard's Almanack*

# Sweet Potato Fries

Contributed by Darnell Gilyard

## Ingredients
3 large sweet potatoes
1 tablespoon baking soda
1½ coffee mugs cornstarch
6 coffee mugs water
1½ teaspoons salt
4 coffee mugs vegetable oil

## Directions
Slice sweet potatoes into 1-inch slices. Now slice these slices into 1½ inch sticks. Bring 4 coffee mugs of water to a boil. Add a tablespoon of baking soda and 1 teaspoon salt to this water. Now you add the sweet potato sticks and bring back to a boil. Boil for 5 minutes. While these are cooking, in a separate bowl, combine 1½ coffee mugs cornstarch and 2 coffee mugs hot water. Mix well. Mixture will be soupy. Make sure all lumps and clumps are out. Drain sweet potatoes and empty pot. Put sweet potatoes in cornstarch slurry and let them soak for a few minutes. Heat a deep fryer to 325° and fry sweet potato sticks until they become golden brown. Add a little salt and enjoy.

> If nature has made you a giver, your hands are born open, and so is your heart. And though there may be times your hands are empty, your heart is always full, and you can give things out of that.
> – Frances Hodgson Burnett

# Sweet & Spicy Pork & Beef

Contributed by Benito Gutierrez

## Ingredients
2 three-ounce beef Ramen noodles
2 coffee mugs hot water
1 jalapeno pepper (1-3-ounce single)
5 heaping tablespoons salad dressing
1/2 of an eight-ounce bag instant rice
1 five-ounce summer sausage
1 two-and-three-quarter-ounce bag pork skins
2 packets fruit punch Kool-Aid (.14-ounce) *

## Directions
Crush Ramen noodles and remove seasoning package from bag. Leave noodles in bag. Combine rice and 1¼ cups of your hot water in a large spread bowl, cover tightly, and let cook for 12-15 minutes. While waiting on rice to cook, dice up summer sausage into small pieces. About 4 minutes before rice is ready, add half the remaining water in each Ramen noodle and use a pen to hold bags closed. Allow these to cook in bags for 4 minutes. Dice the jalapeno pepper while you wait. Once all is ready, add Ramen to rice bowl, along with summer sausage, jalapeno pepper pieces, pork skins, and salad dressing. Once all is mixed well, add your Kool Aid, and mix well again. The flavor is mind-blowing!

*Packages of Kool Aid are equal to 2 tablespoons each.

It is hard for an empty sack to stand upright.
– Benjamin Franklin

# Tea-Markable

Contributed by Roy Lopez

## Ingredients
4 three-ounce chili Ramen noodles
4½ coffee mugs hot water
1 package sliced jalapeno peppers (.6-ounce single)
1 good issue lettuce
1 five-ounce spicy summer sausage
2 two-ounce packages salted peanuts
1 packet lemon iced tea mix* (.14-ounce)

## Directions
Crush Ramen noodles and place all in a large 16-ounce chip bag. Pour in only 4 coffee mugs hot water in this bag. Tie up bag and wrap in a towel. Cook for 10 minutes. While waiting, cut up jalapeno slices into small pieces and chop up lettuce. Dice up summer sausage as well. When Ramen is ready, drain any excess water, combine all remaining ingredients, and mix well. Make sure tea mix is dissolved. Welcome to the remarkable Tea-Markable.

*Package of lemon tea mix is equal to 2 tablespoons

One's dignity may be assaulted, vandalized, and
cruelly mocked, but cannot be taken away
unless it is surrendered.
– Michael J. Fox

# Teriyaki Chicken

Contributed by Ashley Glass

### Ingredients
8 skinless. boneless chicken thighs
1 eight-ounce bottle teriyaki marinade
1 tablespoon vegetable oil
8 tablespoons BBQ sauce
1 small spring onion
1/4 coffee mug sesame seeds
fresh coriander leaves to garnish

### Directions
Open out thigh fillets, place between two baking sheets. Beat chicken until 1½ inches thick. Cut each fillet into 2-3 smaller pieces. Place these pieces in a shallow bowl with the teriyaki marinade and oil. Cover and marinade for 1 hour at room temperature. Preheat BBQ while waiting. Cook chicken on medium heat for 5 minutes, each side. Pour BBQ sauce into pan and allow it to caramelize on the chicken. Remove all from pan and garnish with the sesame seeds and coriander leaves.

> The sages do not consider that making no mistakes is a blessing. They believe, rather, that the great virtue of man lies in his ability to correct his mistakes and continually make a new man of himself.
> – Wang Yang-Ming

# Texas State Chow Mein

Contributed by Bob Leach

### Ingredients

1/2 of an eight-ounce bag instant rice
1½ coffee mugs hot water
2 four-ounce servings vegetables
1 light tablespoon garlic powder
1 four-ounce package turkey bites
soy sauce to taste

### Directions

Combine rice, garlic powder, and hot water in a large spread bowl, cover tightly and let cook for 15 minutes. While waiting, cut up turkey bites and vegetables. Once cook time is complete, add turkey bites and vegetables to bowl and mix well. Now top with soy sauce and eat up.

We should keep in mind that words are like dollar bills:
The more we put in circulation,
the more the currency is devalued.
– Paul Thigpen

# Texas Tuna Melt

Contributed by Troy Traylor

**Ingredients**
1/2 of an eight-ounce bag instant rice
1 coffee mug black beans
2½ coffee mugs hot water
1 four-and-a-quarter-ounce package tuna
2 jalapeno peppers (1.3-ounce singles)
1/4 of a sixteen-ounce bottle squeeze cheese
6 flour tortillas
salt, black pepper, and salsa to taste

**Directions**
Combine rice, black beans, and hot water in a large spread bowl, cover tightly, and allow to cook for 15 minutes. While waiting, cut up jalapeno peppers. If you have a microwave or personal grill, heat/toast flour tortillas. Once cooked, drain any water from rice mixture and drain tuna. Add tuna, pepper pieces, salt, and black pepper to rice bowl and mix well. Coat flour tortillas with some cheese and top with tuna mixture. Roll up in to burritos and tuck one end. Place these in a large chip bag, and double bag. Place bag in a hot pot to heat for 3 hours. Hotter the pot the better. When ready, place your tuna melts in a large spread bowl and top lightly with more cheese and salsa. Your favorite chips and a cold drink will go great with these.

Whoever gossips to you will gossip about you.
– Spanish Proverb

# TJ's Stir Fry

Contributed by Troy Traylor, Jr.

## Ingredients
3 three-ounce spicy vegetable Ramen noodles
2 three-and-a half-ounce packages mackerel
5 tablespoons honey
4-5 tablespoons milk
1/2 five-ounce hot summer sausage
1/2 of a nine-ounce hot pickle
1/4 of a sixteen-ounce bottle squeeze cheese
10 sugar cubes or ten teaspoons of sugar
onion, broccoli, and green pepper to taste

## Directions
Cut up pickle, green pepper, onion, and broccoli and place in a
bowl with the mackerel. Cut up sausage in a large spread bowl
by itself. Crush Ramen in a third large spread bowl and add just
2 seasoning packets and 6 sugar cubes with enough pickle juice
to lightly wet noodles. Place bowl in a microwave on medium
heat for 45 seconds. Stir and add a bit more pickle juice to bowl
and heat another 30 seconds. Noodles should be only half
cooked. Now cover sausage with 1/2 the honey and cook in
microwave on high until brownish-black. Combine sausage bowl,
pickle mixture, and bowl of Ramen and mix well. In a small bowl
or cup, mix the cheese, milk, and 2 tablespoons honey and stir
well. Add 4 crushed sugar cubes and whip until you have a
creamy cheese sauce to pour over the stir fry. To get fancy,
crumb 3 pieces of dried white bread for a bread-crumb topping!

> Speak little, do much.
> – Benjamin Franklin, *Poor Richard's Almanack*

# Tuna Casserole

Contributed by James Campbell, Jr.

**Ingredients**
1 three-ounce shrimp Ramen noodles
1½ coffee mugs hot water
1 four-and-a-quarter-ounce package tuna
2 tablespoons relish*
15 saltine crackers (optional)
1 sleeve snack crackers (optional)

**Directions**
Crush Ramen noodles and place in a large spread bowl with the hot water. Cover tightly and let cook for 5 minutes. Drain off any excess water from Ramen. Drain tuna and slightly crush saltine crackers, combine tuna, salad dressing, relish, and saltine crackers with the Ramen and mix well. Eat this dish as it is or with snack crackers – either way, praise God and eat up!

*If your unit does not sell relish you can make your own with a pickle, pickle juice, a little jalapeno pepper, and some sugar.

> Freedom has its life in the hearts, the actions, the spirit of men, and so it must be daily earned and refreshed – else like a flower cut from its life-giving roots, it will wither and die.
> – Dwight D. Eisenhower (1890-1969),
> 34th U.S. President, 1953-1961

# Tuna Mix

Contributed by Troy Traylor

**Ingredients**
1 nine-ounce dill pickle (any flavor)
2 three-ounce chicken Ramen noodles
1/4 of a sixteen-ounce bottle squeeze cheese
1½ coffee mugs full of party mix
2 packets ranch dressing* (1.5 ounces)
2 four-and-a-quarter-ounce packages tuna
2 coffee mugs hot water
2 tablespoons onion flakes (optional)
8 flour tortillas

**Directions**
Cut up pickles into small pieces and drain water from tuna. Crush both Ramen noodles and add just one seasoning packet to a large spread bowl with the hot water. Cover tightly and let cook for just 5 minutes. Drain off any remaining water and add cheese, onion flakes, and party mix to bowl and stir well. Once well mixed, add both tuna packages and stir again. Allow this to set for 30 minutes so chips soften, and flavors combine. Now spoon mixture onto the flour tortillas and roll up. Place 4 in a spread bowl and cover with one ranch dressing. Repeat with last four and enjoy a meal with your cellie or an associate. Save last seasoning packet for another dish.

*Packages of ranch dressing are equal to 2 tablespoons each.

> Life is tough – it's tougher if you're stupid!
> – John Wayne

# Tuna Noodle Casserole

Contributed by Troy Traylor, Jr.

**Ingredients**
4 three-ounce chicken Ramen Noodles
3/4 coffee mug instant milk
4½ coffee mugs hot water
2 four-and-three-quarter-ounce packages tuna
2 tablespoons butter
1 one-and-three-quarter-ounce bottle onion flakes
1 three-ounce package dehydrated tomato and green chili
1 three-ounce package mushrooms (if available)
1 coffee mug peas
1/4 of a sixteen-ounce bottle squeeze cheese
2 tablespoons soy sauce
salt and black pepper to taste

**Directions**
This is another recipe perfect for an Ad-Seg prisoner. Crush Ramen and place all in a large spread bowl. Add the instant milk and 4 cups hot water to bowl and stir to dissolve the milk. Add 2 seasonings and stir again. Now cover bowl tightly and let cook for about 6 minutes. Ramen will cook and still have creamy milk in the bowl. Drain the tuna. Set Soy sauce aside, combine all remaining ingredients, and thoroughly mix. Once all is mixed pour soy sauce over top and dig in. Set remaining seasonings aside for another recipe.

Always do what you are afraid to do.
– Ralph Waldo Emerson

# Turkey Pecan Salad

Contributed by Rene Sanchez

## Ingredients
2 coffee mugs pecans
3 stalks celery
1 teaspoon Worcestershire
1 light teaspoon white pepper
1 pound of cooked turkey breast
1 coffee mug mayo
1 tablespoon sugar
1 bed of lettuce

## Directions
Toast the pecans in the oven at 350° for 10 minutes. While waiting, cube up turkey breast and chop celery coarsely. Once all this is done, in a medium bowl combine and toss these three ingredients. Set lettuce aside for a moment and in a small bowl combine the mayo, Worcestershire, sugar, and white pepper. Mix all well. Now add this to turkey bowl and mix well again. Now make your bed of lettuce and top with the turkey mixture.

Without inspiration the best powers of the mind remain dormant. There is a fuel in us which needs to be ignited with sparks.
– Johann Gottfried Von Herder

# Vienna-Chili Cheese Dog Wraps

Contributed by Troy Traylor

## Ingredients
1 eleven-and-a-quarter-ounce package chili with beans
2 three-ounce packages Vienna sausage
1 package chili seasoning from Ramen
1/4 of a sixteen-ounce bottle squeeze cheese
1 ten-ounce package flour tortillas
mustard to taste

## Directions
Leave Vienna sausages whole and combine with chili package, in a rice bag. Add chili seasoning to bag and lightly stir. Place bag in a hot pot to heat for 2 hours, lightly stirring occasionally. When cook time is complete, spread some squeeze cheese on flour tortillas and line with a Vienna sausage and some chili. Top with mustard and roll up. Repeat until ingredients are exhausted.

> " Nothing contributes so much to tranquilize the mind
> as a steady purpose – a point on which the soul
> may fix its intellectual eye.
> – Mary Shelley

# Special Days for the Foodie

July
(1st): National Gingersnap Day
(2nd): National Anisette Day
(3rd): National Chocolate Wafer Day
(4th): National Barbecue Day, Caesar Salad Day
(5th): National Apple Turnover Day
(6th): National Fried Chicken Day
(7th): National Strawberry Sundae Day, National Macaroni Day
(8th): National Chocolate with Almonds Day
(9th): National Sugar Cookie Day
(10th): National Piña Colada Day, "Pick Blueberries" Day
(11th): National Blueberry Muffin Day, National Mojito Day
(12th): National Pecan Pie Day
(13th): National French Fry Day
(14th): National Grand Marnier Day
(15th): National Gummy Worm Day
(16th): National Ice Cream Day, National Corn Fritter Day
(17th): National Peach Ice Cream Day
(18th): National Caviar Day
(19th): National Daiquiri Day
(20th): National Ice Cream Sundae Day, National Lollipop Day
(21st): National Crème Brûlée Day, National Junk Food Day
(22nd): National Penuche Day
(23rd): National Vanilla Ice Cream Day, Official Hot Dog Day
(24th): National Tequila Day
(25th): National Hot Fudge Sundae Day
(26th): National Bagel-fest, National Coffee Milkshake Day
(27th): National Scotch Day
(28th): National Milk Chocolate Day, National Hamburger Day
(29th): National Lasagna Day, National Chicken Wing Day
(30th): National Cheesecake Day
(31st): National Raspberry Cake Day, National Cotton Candy
Day

# Section VI:
# A Few Delicious Pizzas

# Amazing Pizza

Contributed by Tammy Wise

## Ingredients
3 tablespoons butter
1 four-ounce package turkey bites
1 eight-ounce package Mexican beef
3 tablespoons hot sauce
1/4 of a sixteen-ounce bottle squeeze cheese
1 three-and-a-half-ounce package pepperoni slices
1 ten-ounce package flour tortillas
2 jalapeno peppers (1.3-ounce singles)
1/3 of a twenty-ounce bottle Ketchup
1 teaspoon season all
1 four-ounce serving pineapples from tray

## Directions
You will need to be at a unit that has a microwave or have a personal grill. Butter tortillas on one side and cook in a microwave for 30-40 seconds. Flip over and repeat this step. Should be on the crispy side. Dice up turkey bites and jalapeno peppers. In a spread bowl combine turkey bites, jalapeno peppers, and Mexican beef. In a cup mix ketchup and hot sauce together and coat half the flour tortillas. Sprinkle all with season all. Divide meat mixture and cover half the tortillas. Top off all with squeeze cheese, pineapples, and pepperoni. Put other tortilla shell on top and press down. Unless you're hungry, better invite an associate. Amazing for sure!

He that will not reflect is a ruined man.
– Asian Proverb

# BBQ Pizza

Contributed by Troy Traylor

## Ingredients

3 three-ounce beef Ramen noodles
2¾ coffee mugs hot water
1 two-and-three-quarter-ounce bag pork skins
1/3 sixteen-ounce bag corn chips
1 four-ounce package turkey bites
1/4 of a sixteen-ounce bottle squeeze cheese
1/4 of an eleven-ounce bag Cheese Puffs
BBQ sauce to taste

## Directions

Crush Ramen noodles and corn chips and combine both in a large (16-ounce) chip bag. Add hot water to bag and knead until most water is absorbed. Flatten out mixture in this chip bag and even out. Wrap in newspaper or a towel and set aside for 15 minutes. Dice turkey bites and crush pork skins into a fine powder. Once cook time is complete, unwrap pizza and cut bag open length wise. Coat the pizza with the squeeze cheese and top with pork skins and turkey bites. Cover all with BBQ sauce. Now lightly crush Cheese Puffs and decorate pizza. Sprinkle with 1 seasoning from Ramen and leave the other 2 for another recipe. Enjoy with your favorite drink.

> We are either progressing or retrograding all the while; there is no such thing as remaining stationary in this life.
> – James Freeman Clarke

# Papa J'S Personal Pizza

Contributed by John Clarke

## Ingredients
3 flour tortillas
4-5 tablespoons ketchup
1 tablespoon chili garlic sauce
1 teaspoon onion powder
1/2 teaspoon garlic powder
1 nice-size chicken quarter
1 one-and-a-half-ounce package ranch dressing*
1 jalapeno pepper (1.3-ounce single)
squeeze cheese to taste

## Directions
Heat up the 3 tortillas in a microwave or your personal grill. Combine ketchup and chili garlic sauce in a cup and mix well. Add onion powder and garlic powder to cup and mix that in. Now shred up your chicken quarter. Layer one tortilla with cheese and cover cheese with your sauce. Now put half the shredded chicken on this one. Top with second tortilla and repeat steps above. When you top off with third tortilla, cover this one with a little more cheese. Pour ranch over this and decorate with diced jalapeno peppers.

*Package of ranch dressing is equal to 2 tablespoons.

It is not what a man does that determines whether his work is sacred or secular, but why he does it.
– A.W. Tozer

# Pizza-Pizza

Contributed by Michael Henry

### Ingredients
1 five-ounce summer sausage
1 thirteen-ounce box snack crackers
4 tablespoons hot water
5 tablespoons chili garlic sauce
1 two-ounce package cream cheese
1 seven-ounce package chicken chunks
1 sleeve saltine crackers
1/2 of a twenty-ounce bottle ketchup
2 jalapeno peppers (1.3-ounce singles)
1/4 of a sixteen-ounce bottle squeeze cheese

### Directions
Dice up summer sausage into small pieces and shred chicken chunks. Place both meats together in chicken chunks package and place in a hot pot to heat for 1 hour. While waiting, crush up all crackers and place in a large sixteen-ounce chip bag. Add hot water to bag and knead into your dough. Flatten out dough in chip bag and even out. Cut bag open length wise and allow to air dry while meats heat. Once all is ready, mix ketchup with chili garlic sauce and coat dough with this. Top with meat mixture. Dice up jalapeno peppers and spread evenly over meat mixture. Now drizzle your pizza with cream cheese and squeeze cheese. Perfect meal for 1.

Our life is what our thoughts make it.
– Marcus Aurelius

# Stuffed Crust Pizza

Contributed by Troy Traylor

### Ingredients
1 eleven-and-a-quarter-ounce package chili no beans
1/2 of an eleven-ounce bag cheese puffs
1/4 of a fifteen-ounce bag refried beans*
1 four-ounce package turkey bites
1/4 of a sixteen-ounce bottle squeeze cheese
1 three-and-a-half-ounce package pepperoni slices
1/2 of a sixteen-ounce bag corn chips
3 three-ounce chili Ramen noodles
4 coffee mugs hot water
2 jalapeno peppers (1.3-ounce singles)
hot sauce to taste

### Directions
Two hot pots are best for this one, set to the highest temperature possible. Rinse meat package and heat in a hot pot. Crush corn chips, cheese puffs, and Ramen noodles fairly fine. In a large 16-ounce chip bag, combine corn chips, cheese puffs, Ramen noodles, refried beans, 1 seasoning packet (save the other 2 for another dish), and hot water. Knead and flatten out in the bag, wrap bag in newspaper or towel, and set aside to cook for 15 minutes. While waiting dice turkey bites and jalapeno pepper. Once cooked, cut chip bag open length wise. Spread layers evenly in this order: Squeeze cheese, chili, turkey bites, jalapeno peppers, hot sauce, and pepperoni slices. Incredibly delicious!

*Refried beans will be equal to a heavy 3/4 coffee mug.

Success is a series of glorious defeats.
– Mahatma Ghandi

# Special Days for the Foodie

August

(1st): National Raspberry Cream Pie Day

(2nd): National Ice Cream Sandwich Day

(3rd): National Watermelon Day, National IPA Day

(4th): National Chocolate Chip Cookie Day

(5th): National Oyster Day

(6th): National Root Beer Float Day

(7th): Raspberries and Cream Day

(8th): National Frozen Custard Day, National Zucchini Day

(9th): National Rice Pudding Day

(10th): National S'mores Day, National Banana Split Day

(11th): National Panini Day, National Raspberry Tart Day

(12th): National Julienne Fries Day

(13th): National Filet Mignon Day

(14th): National Creamsicle Day

(15th): National Lemon Meringue Pie Day (Julia Child's Birthday)

(16th): National Rum Day, National Bratwurst Day

(17th): National Vanilla Custard Day

(18th): National Ice Cream Pie Day

(19th): National Hot & Spicy Food Day

(20th): National Chocolate Pecan Pie Day

(21st): National Sweet Tea Day

(22nd): National Pecan Torte Day, National "Eat a Peach" Day

(23rd): National Cuban Sandwich Day, National Sponge Cake Day

(24th): National Peach Pie Day

(25th): National Whiskey Sour Day

(26th): National Cherry Popsicle Day

(27th): National Pots de Crème Day, National Burger Day

(28th): National Cherry Turnovers Day

(29th): National Chop Suey

(30th): National Toasted Marshmallow Day

(31st): National Trail Mix Day

September

(1st): National Gyro Day

(2nd): National "Grits for Breakfast" Day, International Bacon Day

(3rd): National Welsh Rarebit Day, National Baby Back Ribs Day

(4th): National Macadamia Nut Day

(5th): National Cheese Pizza Day

(6th): National Coffee Ice Cream Day

(7th): National Beer Lover's Day

(8th): National Date-Nut Bread Day

(9th): National "I Love Food" Day

(10th): National Hot Dog Day

(11th): National Hot Cross Bun Day

(12th): National Chocolate Milkshake Day

(13th): National Peanut Day

(14th): National Cream-Filled Doughnut Day

(15th): National Double Cheeseburger Day, National Linguini Day

(16th): National Cinnamon-Raisin Bread Day

(17th): National Apple Dumpling Day, National Monte Cristo Day

(18th): National Play-Dough Day, National Cheeseburger Day

(19th): National Butterscotch Pudding Day

(20th): National Punch Day, National Rum Punch Day

(21st): National Pecan Cookie Day

(22nd): National Ice Cream Cone Day

(23rd): National White Chocolate Day

(24th): National Cherries Jubilee Day

(25th): National Lobster Day, National Food Service Workers Day

(26th): National Key Lime Pie Day

(27th): National Chocolate Milk Day

(28th): National Strawberry Cream Pie Day

(29th): National Coffee Day, National Mocha Day

(30th): National Mulled Cider Day

# Section VII:
# Mexican Delights For All Occasions

# Acapulco Burrito

Contributed by Isidro Teran

### Ingredients

2 flour tortillas
1/4 coffee mug refried beans
1/4 coffee mug hot water
1/2 of a nine-ounce dill pickle
2 tablespoons squeeze cheese
1 three-ounce chili Ramen noodles
1 three-and-a-half-ounce package sardines
1 jalapeno pepper (1.3-ounce single)
1/4 coffee mug party mix
1 one-and-a-half-ounce package ranch dressing

### Directions

In an empty 16-ounce chip bag make a taco shell by placing 2 flour tortillas lengthwise, overlapped by about half, down the long side of the bag. Crush the Ramen noodles in their bag, add refried beans, and shake. Evenly pour this mixture over tortillas. Put the sardines on top of Ramen. Now pour the hot water over this mixture. Twist this bag closed. As you twist, these ingredients will begin to roll into a large burrito. Once rolled, tie off bag, wrap in a towel, and set aside 15 minutes to cook. While waiting, dice the jalapeno peppers and pickle. Crush party mix. Once cooked, cut bag open and place burrito in a large spread bowl and top in this order: squeeze cheese, ranch dressing, party mix, jalapeno pepper, and pickle. That's how it's done in Acapulco!

*Package of ranch dressing are equal to 2 tablespoons.

Make each day your masterpiece. – John Wooden

# Basic Burritos

Contributed by David Harris

### Ingredients
3/4 coffee mug instant rice
2½ coffee mugs hot water
3 tablespoons salad dressing
1 coffee mug instant chili beans
1 two-and-three-quarter-ounce bag pork skins
3 flour tortillas
habanera and squeeze cheese to taste

### Directions
Combine rice, instant chili, and hot water in a large spread bowl.
Mix well, cover tightly, and let cook for 12-15 minutes. Lightly
crush pork skins. Once cooked, set flour tortillas aside and
combine all remaining ingredients. Mix well. Now spoon mixture
onto flour tortillas and roll into your burritos. Grab your favorite
chips and a cold drink.

> The question for each man to settle is not what he would do if
> he had means, time, influence, and educational advantages;
> the question is what he will do with the things he has. The
> moment a young man ceases to dream or to bemoan his lack
> of opportunities and resolutely looks his conditions in the face,
> and resolves to change them, he lays the cornerstone of solid
> and honorable success.
> – Hamilton Wright Mabie

# Beef and Potato Burritos

Contributed by Troy Traylor

### Ingredients
1 eleven-and-a-quarter-ounce package chili no beans
1/2 of a nine-ounce dill pickle
2 jalapeno peppers (1.3-ounce singles)
1 eight-ounce bag jalapeno chips
1 coffee mug refried beans
1½ coffee mugs hot water
1/3 sixteen-ounce bottle squeeze cheese
1 ten-ounce package flour tortillas
2 packages cream cheese/ranch (optional)
hot sauce to taste

### Directions
Rinse meat package and heat in a high-temperature hot pot. While cooking, dice pickle and jalapeno peppers and crush chips in bag. Add pickle, peppers, and refried beans to chip bag and shake well. Once meat is hot, pour it into chip bag with the hot water and knead well. Allow water and chili to absorb and flatten out mixture in bag like a pizza. Wrap bag in a towel and set aside for 15 minutes. Afterward, coat the flour tortillas with squeeze cheese and cut bag open length wise. Cut mixture in bag in 2 or 3-inch strips. Place these strips on tortillas and roll up. Place 4 burritos in a rice bag and place bag in a hot pot to heat for 2 hours. Once cooked, place 4 burritos in a large spread bowl and top with hot sauce. You can add cream cheese or ranch on top if you wish. Repeat cooking steps with rest. Two hot pots really help.

> Hear no ill of a friend, nor speak any of an enemy.
> – Ben Franklin

# Beef Tip Tacos

Contributed by Vernon Miller

### Ingredients
1 eight-ounce package beef tips
1 eleven-and-a-quarter-ounce package BBQ beef
2 jalapeno peppers (1.3-ounce singles)
1 package chili seasoning from Ramen
1 three-ounce bag Salsa Verde chips
1/3 of a sixteen-ounce bottle squeeze cheese
8 flour tortillas
habanera sauce to taste

### Directions
Dice up beef tips and combine with BBQ beef in a large spread bowl. Dice the jalapeno peppers and add to bowl, along with chili seasoning. Crush the chips and add these to bowl and stir well. Coat your flour tortillas with squeeze cheese and top with BBQ mixture. Fold in half to create your tacos. Place 4 in a rice bag and place bag in a hot pot to heat for 2 hours. Once done, place 4 tacos in your spread bowl and top with habanera sauce. Repeat these steps with final 4. Two hot pots are best to have all done at once.

> For the good or the ill your conversation is your advertisement. Every time you open your mouth you let men look inside your mind.
> – Bruce Burton

# Beefy Swine Tacos

Contributed by Troy Traylor

### Ingredients
2 three-ounce packages spam
1 eleven-and-a-quarter-ounce package chili with beans
1/2 of an eight-ounce bag BBQ chips
2 tablespoons squeeze cheese
1 teaspoon garlic powder
1 teaspoon onion powder
1 ten-ounce package flour tortillas
habanera to taste

### Directions
Dice spam into tiny pieces
and place all in a large spread
bowl. Pour chili into bowl. Crush
chips lightly and stir into bowl. Now add your cheese, garlic
powder, and onion powder. Mix thoroughly. Spoon mixture onto
flour tortillas and roll up. Place 4 in rice bag and place in a hot
pot to heat for 2 hours. When cook time is complete, place all 4
in a spread bowl and top with habanera sauce. Repeat until all is
gone. Two hot pots work best.

If you would not be forgotten, as soon as you are
dead and rotten, either write things worth reading,
or do things worth writing.
– Benjamin Franklin

# Big House Tamales

Contributed by Jesus Morales

## Ingredients
1 loaf white bread
2 three-ounce bags hot Cheetos
6 tablespoons hot water
1/2 of a nine-ounce dill pickle
2 jalapeno peppers (1.3-ounce singles)
1 five-ounce summer sausage
squeeze cheese and salsa to taste

## Directions

Remove crust from bread and break bread into small pieces. Crush both bags of hot Cheetos into a powder. Place all in a large spread bowl. Add hot water to bowl and knead into a dough-type substance. Roll this dough out on plastic on your bunk. Allow to sit for 1 hour to absorb moisture. While waiting, dice pickle, jalapeno peppers, and summer sausage. Once dry time is complete, coat dough with squeeze cheese and top on one edge with the summer sausage mixture. Now carefully roll dough over mixture. Roll with pressure to keep tight. Pinch edge once done to close. Now you have one huge tamale. Top with salsa and enjoy. If you prefer to have several small tamales, just cut dough into equal parts and follow directions with the "stuffing."

The gem cannot be polished without friction,
nor man perfected without trial.
– Confucius

# Bo's Tamale Pie

Contributed by Chris Killman

## Ingredients
1 eight-ounce package Mexican beef
2 jalapeno peppers (1.3-ounce singles)
1 good size tomato (if available)
1 coffee mug hot water
1 ten-ounce package corn tortillas
1 eleven-and-a-quarter-ounce chili no beans
1 heavy teaspoon taco seasoning
1/4 medium size onion*
3/4 coffee mug refried beans
2 two-ounce packages cream cheese*
2 four-ounce servings corn from tray
habanera and squeeze cheese to taste

## Directions
Rinse both meat packages and heat in a hot pot. Hotter pots are best. Add the taco seasoning to chili package while it heats. While cooking, dice the jalapenos, onion, and tomato. Also cook refried beans and leave pretty thick. Tear up corn tortillas into 4 per tortilla. When meat packages are ready combine all ingredients in the spread bowl and mix thoroughly. Top with habanera sauce and dig in.

*If no onions are available on your unit, sub with a few tablespoons of onion powder.

*Packages of cream cheese are equal to 4 tablespoons each.

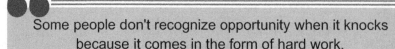

Some people don't recognize opportunity when it knocks because it comes in the form of hard work.
– H.L. Mencken

# Buck's Burritos

Contributed by Charlie Buckland

**Ingredients**

1 coffee mug brown rice
3/4 coffee mug instant black beans
2½ coffee mugs hot water
1/2 of a three-ounce package dehydrated tomato and green chili
1 seven-ounce package chicken chunks
3 tablespoons parmesan cheese
1 cup corn (from tray)
4 flour tortillas
salt, black pepper, and (optional) squeeze cheese to taste

**Directions**

In a large spread bowl combine rice, black beans, tomato and green chili mix, and hot water. Mix well, cover bowl tightly, and cook for 15 minutes. While waiting, drain and shred chicken chunks. Once cook time is complete, set the flour tortillas aside and combine all remaining ingredients. Mix well and spoon mixture onto tortillas. Roll or fold.

> To win one hundred victories in
> one hundred battles is not the acme of skill.
> To subdue the enemy without fighting is the acme of skill.
> – Sun Tzu, Chinese strategist

# Cheesy Chicken Enchiladas

Contributed by Troy Traylor

## Ingredients
1/2 of an eight-ounce bag instant rice
1¼ coffee mugs hot water
2 jalapeno peppers (1.3-ounce singles)
1 seven-ounce package chicken chunks
1/4 of an eight-ounce bag jalapeno chips
1 teaspoon taco seasoning
1 teaspoon chicken seasoning from Ramen
1/4 of a sixteen-ounce bottle squeeze cheese
6 corn tortillas
8 tablespoons salsa

## Directions
Combine rice and hot water in a large spread bowl, cover tightly, and cook for 10-12 minutes. While waiting, dice jalapeno pepper, shred chicken, and lightly crush chips. When rice is ready, drain any excess water and stir in jalapeno peppers, chicken chunks, jalapeno chips, taco seasoning, and chicken seasoning. Stir well. Cover corn tortillas with cheese and spoon on chip mixture. Roll these up and place 3 in a rice bag. Place bag in a hot pot to cook for 3 hours. Once cooked, place the 3 in a spread bowl and cover with salsa. If you do not have 2 hot pots just repeat cooking steps.

Whatever may happen, every kind of misfortune
is to be overcome by bearing it.
– Virgil

Troy Traylor

# Chicharron a La Barras

Contributed by Gilbert Martinez

### Ingredients
2 three-ounce chili Ramen noodles
1 twelve-ounce V-8 juice
1 coffee mug refried beans
1 ten-ounce package flour tortillas
2 two-and-three-quarter-ounce bags pork skins
2 jalapeno peppers (1.3-ounce singles)
1/4 of a sixteen ounce bottle squeeze cheese

### Directions
Crush Ramen and pork skins. Combine Ramen and 1½ pork skins in a large, 16-ounce chip bag and set aside a few minutes. Open V-8 juice and place in a hot pot to heat. Hotter pots work best. Once V-8 is hot, pour 3/4 can into Ramen mixture. Tie off bag and wrap in a towel for 10 minutes. While waiting, dice jalapeno peppers and place refried beans in a bowl. Pour remaining V-8 in bowl, cover tightly, and cook for 10 minutes. Once all is ready, add jalapeno peppers to Ramen mixture. Cover the tortillas with squeeze cheese, a thin layer of refried beans, and Ramen mixture. Roll these up and place 4 in a bowl. Top with salsa and sprinkle with remaining pork skins.

> Character cannot be developed in ease and quiet.
> Only through experiences of trial and suffering can the
> soul be strengthened, vision cleared, ambition inspired,
> and success achieved.
> – Helen Keller

# Chicken Tostadas

Contributed by Sherry Perez

## Ingredients
1 large tomato
4 good-size chicken breast
3 coffee mugs hot water
6 tostadas
1 small onion
1 three-ounce Cajun chicken Ramen noodles
2 coffee mugs instant chili beans
1 coffee mug shredded cheddar cheese
1/2 coffee mug French onion dip
lettuce and salsa to taste

## Directions
Dice tomato and onion. Shred chicken breast and grill until cooked. Crush Ramen noodles and place all in a medium size bowl. Add 1 coffee mug hot water to bowl, cover tightly, and cook for 5 minutes. While this is cooking place refried beans into a separate, microwave-safe bowl, with 2 coffee mugs hot water. Place this bowl in a microwave. Cover and cook on high for 5 minutes. Drain any remaining water from Ramen. Combine Ramen, instant chili beans, and chicken. Mix well. Grab 3 of the tostadas and cover with Ramen mixture. Top with tomato, onion, cheddar cheese, lettuce, French onion dip, and salsa. You can now top with left over tostadas or you can repeat steps on last three.

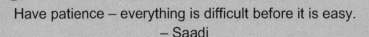

Have patience – everything is difficult before it is easy.
– Saadi

# Corny Enchiladas

Contributed by Troy Traylor

### Ingredients
1/2 of a sixteen-ounce bag corn chips
1/2 of a sixteen-ounce bag tortilla chips
1 twelve-ounce V-8 juice
2 eight-ounce packages Mexican beef
1 packet chili seasoning from Ramen
1 teaspoon taco seasoning
2 jalapeno peppers (1.3-ounce singles)
1/4 of a sixteen-ounce bottle squeeze cheese
1 two-ounce package cream cheese*
hot sauce to taste

### Directions
This recipe is a little
tricky for beginners.
First, crush all the
chips into a fine
powder and
combine them in

one large chip bag. Carefully add small amounts of V-8 juice to
the bag (it may help to heat the V-8 a few degrees), kneading
the mixture so that it is just moist enough for the chips to stick
together. You want this mixture to roll up without breaking, so
you will use about 1/4 of the can of juice. Flatten out the mixture
in the chip bag into a pizza shape. Cut the bag open length wise
and use a can or jar to roll out the mixture somewhat thin. Allow
this to dry while you are preparing the rest of the recipe. Using a
rice bag, combine both packages of Mexican beef with the chili
and taco seasonings. Place this bag in a hot pot to heat for 1
hour. Now dice the jalapeno peppers into tiny pieces and cut the
chip mixture into 4-inch squares. When all is ready, coat all the

squares with squeeze cheese. Spoon meat mixture on each square and roll them into enchiladas. Place 4 or more enchiladas into a rice bag and place the bag into a hot pot to heat for 1 hour. When cooking is complete, place the enchiladas in a large spread bowl and drizzle with cream cheese, decorate this dish with  jalapeno pieces and then dash with hot sauce. You will write home about this one!

*Packages of cream cheese are equal to 4 tablespoons each.

To laugh often and much; to win the respect of intelligent people ...; to earn the appreciation of honest critics and endure the betrayal of false friends; ... to find the best in others; to leave the world a little better; whether by a healthy child, a garden patch or a redeemed social condition; to know even one life has breathed easier because you have lived. This is the meaning of success.
– Ralph Waldo Emerson

Troy Traylor

# Eric's Enchiladas

Contributed by Eric Decker

## Ingredients

1 five-ounce summer sausage
2 jalapeno peppers (1.3-ounce singles)
1 two-and-three-quarter-ounce bag pork skins
1 eleven-and-a-quarter-ounce package chili no beans
1 eleven-and-a-quarter-ounce package chili with beans
1 eight-ounce package beef tips
1 eight-ounce package Mexican beef
1 chili seasoning packet from Ramen
1 ten-ounce package flour tortillas
1/3 of a sixteen-ounce bottle
squeeze cheese
5 tablespoons salsa

## Directions

Dice summer sausage and
jalapeno peppers. Lightly
crush pork skins. Combine all
meat packages, summer
sausage, pork skins, and chili

seasoning in a large spread bowl and mix well. Spoon mixture
onto flour tortillas and roll up. Place 4 in a rice bag and set in hot
pot for 3 hours to cook. Two hot pots work best for heating.
Repeat these steps until all are gone. When each bag is ready,
place 4 enchiladas in a spread bowl and top with cheese and
salsa. Now decorate with pepper pieces and enjoy with a
favorite drink and chips.

The nearer the dawn the darker the night.
– Longfellow

# Fish Tacos

Contributed by Terry Millican

## Ingredients
1 three-ounce chicken Ramen noodles
1½ coffee mugs hot water
1 jalapeno pepper (1.3-ounce single)
1/2 of a nine-ounce pickle (any flavor)
1 three-and-a-half-ounce package mackerel
2½-3 tablespoons salad dressing
1/2 of an onion *or* 1½ tablespoons of onion powder
1 coffee mug jalapeno chips (crushed)
3 flour tortillas
squeeze cheese to taste

## Directions
This is a quick and simple recipe. Lightly crush Ramen and put in a large spread bowl with the hot water. Cover tightly and cook for 10 minutes. While cooking, dice jalapeno pepper and pickle. Drain Ramen and add jalapeno pepper, pickle, mackerel, squeeze cheese, salad dressing, and the onion/onion powder. Mix well. Now add in Ramen seasoning and mix again. Crush jalapeno chips and top. Divide mixture into thirds for your tacos. See that: three nice tacos in just 10 minutes.

> We may encounter many defeats,
> but we must not be defeated
> – Maya Angelou

# Frito Pie

Contributed by Joseph Linden

### Ingredients
1 coffee mug refried beans
1 coffee mug hot water
2 jalapeno peppers (1.3-ounce singles)
1 three-ounce bag cheese curls
3 coffee mugs corn chips
squeeze cheese to taste

### Directions
In a large spread bowl combine refried beans and hot water.
Cover tightly and cook for 10 minutes. While waiting, dice up
jalapeno peppers and crush cheese curls. When beans are
ready, combine all ingredients and mix well. Nice treat with your
favorite cold drink.

The more brutal your methods,
the more bitter you will make your opponents,
with the natural result of hardening the
resistance you are trying to overcome.
– Sir Basil Liddell Hart, British military strategist

# Frito Pie II

Anonymous contribution

## Ingredients
2 five-ounce summer sausages
1 nine-ounce dill pickle
3 single serving pepper jack cheese sticks
1 three-and-a-half-ounce package pepperoni slices
4 three-ounce beef Ramen noodles
2 coffee mugs refried beans
7½ coffee mugs hot water
1 four-ounce tub jalapeno cheddar cheese
1 sixteen-ounce bag chili cheese Fritos

## Directions
Dice the summer sausage, dill pickle, cheese sticks, and pepperoni slices. Crush Ramen noodles in package. In a large spread bowl, combine the Ramen and refried beans. Add hot water to bowl, cover tightly, and cook for 8 minutes. After cooking is complete, set cheddar cheese and Fritos aside, combine all remaining ingredients and mix well. In a separate spread bowl

layer 1/4 bag of Fritos with 1/4 of meat mixture on top. Repeat until all Fritos and meat mixture is gone. Now pour cheese over the top. Cover your door and eat up. You will not want to share this one!

> All that is necessary for the triumph of evil
> is that good men do nothing.
> – Edmund Burke

Troy Traylor

# Mr. T's Burritos

Contributed by Troy Traylor

### Ingredients
2¼ coffee mugs hot water
1/2 coffee mug instant rice
1/2 teaspoon season-all
1 teaspoon onion powder
2 two-ounce packages salted peanuts
2 three-ounce beef Ramen noodles
2 one-ounce fruit sticks
2 four-ounce packages turkey bites
1/2 teaspoon garlic powder
6 flour tortillas
1 package chili seasoning from Ramen
picante sauce and squeeze cheese to taste

### Directions
You will only use 1 beef seasoning packet in this recipe. Save other for another recipe. Crush Ramen lightly. Combine Ramen and rice in a large spread bowl. Crush fruit sticks and add to bowl. Now add your water to bowl. Stir for a minute, cover tightly, and cook for 10 minutes. While waiting, dice turkey bites into small pieces. When cooked drain any excess water. Add the turkey bites, onion powder, garlic powder, season-all, squeeze cheese, and peanuts to bowl and mix well. Spoon mixture onto tortillas and roll up. Place these in your spread bowl and top off with picante sauce and chili seasoning. Makes an incredible meal.

"Fall seven times, stand up eight. – Japanese Proverb"

# Nach-Yo Average Prison Dip

Contributed by Robert Patnoude

### Ingredients

1 eleven-and-a-quarter-ounce package chili with beans
2 three-ounce beef Ramen noodles
1 five-ounce spicy summer sausage
1 medium size onion
1 large tomato *or* 2 medium
4 jalapeno peppers (1.3-ounce singles)
1 four-ounce tub jalapeno cheddar cheese
1 eight-ounce bag bacon potato skins

### Directions

Rinse meat package and cook in a hot pot for 1 hour. During this time, crush Ramen lightly, place in a large spread bowl, and set aside. Now dice summer sausage, onion, tomato(s), and jalapeno peppers. Combine the diced ingredients together in a microwave safe bowl and place bowl in microwave to grill for 3 minutes. Make sure you cover with a napkin to avoid a mess. Stir half way through. Grease from summer sausage will serve as a juice. Once this is done put all on top of Ramen. Once chili package is hot, pour this over Ramen and place bowl back in a microwave on high for another 90 seconds. Noodles will cook. Remove from microwave and pour cheese over the top. Eat with your bacon potato skins. Wow, this is delish.

No gains without pains.
– Ben Franklin, *Poor Richard's Almanack*

# One True Burrito

Contributed by Roy Lopez

**Ingredients**
2 three-ounce chili Ramen noodles
3 coffee mugs hot water
1 packet chili Ramen seasoning
1/2 coffee mug refried beans
1/4 coffee mug rice
1 five-ounce summer sausage
2 packages sliced jalapeno peppers (.6-ounce)
1 two-and-three-quarter-ounce bag pork skins
1 three-ounce bag Cheetos
3 tablespoons salad dressing
nice shot squeeze cheese
1 one-and-a-half-ounce package ranch dressing
onion, bell pepper, and tomato to taste

**Directions**
Crush the Ramen noodles and place them in a large, 16-ounce chip bag. Add 1½ coffee mugs of hot water to the bag and knead until the water is absorbed. Flatten out the Ramen in chip bag into the shape of a pizza and wrap it in a towel for 15 minutes. While waiting, combine 1 seasoning packet, refried beans, rice, and 1½ coffee mugs of water in a large spread bowl. Cover tightly and set aside while Ramen cooks. In the meantime, dice the summer sausage,

jalapeno slices, onion, bell pepper, and tomato. Crush the pork skins and Cheetos. When Ramen is ready, cut bag length wise and cover with salad dressing and squeeze cheese. Now set aside ranch dressing, combine all the remaining ingredients, and mix well. Spread this mixture out evenly on just 1/4 of the Ramen, leaving an inch from the edges uncovered. Now carefully roll up the Ramen around these ingredients, using a little pressure as you roll. This will be a big burrito when you are done. Pour ranch dressing over it and enjoy One True Burrito.

*Packages of ranch dressing are equal to 2 tablespoons each.

We are either the masters or the victims of our attitudes. It is a matter of personal choice. Who we are today is the result of choices we made yesterday. Tomorrow, we will become what we choose today. To change means to choose to change.
– John Maxwell

# Orange Chicken Burritos

Contributed by Troy Traylor

### Ingredients

1 twelve-ounce orange juice
1/2 coffee mug brown rice
1½ coffee mugs refried beans
1 seven-ounce package chicken chunks
2 jalapeno peppers (1.3-ounce singles)
1 package chicken seasoning from Ramen
4 flour tortillas
squeeze cheese to taste

### Directions

Slightly open orange juice and set can in a hot pot to heat. High-temperature pots work best. Combine rice and refried beans in a large spread bowl while you wait. Drain and shred chicken chunks and dice jalapeno peppers as well. Once juice is good and hot, pour into rice mixture and cover bowl tightly. Allow this to cook for 15 minutes. Once cook time is complete, set tortillas aside and combine all remaining ingredients. Mix well and spoon onto tortillas. Roll up and dig in. If you want to add a little orange Kool Aid (2-3 tablespoons) or orange electrolyte (3/4 tablespoon) it will help boost flavor. This is really good.

> People are like stained glass windows. They sparkle and shine when the sun is out, but when the darkness sets in, their beauty is revealed only if there is a light from within.
> – Elizabeth Kubler Ross

# Spicy Pork Burritos

Contributed by Vernon Miller

**Ingredients**
2 three-ounce packages spam
3 tablespoons hot water
1/4 of a nine-ounce dill pickle
4 tablespoons squeeze cheese
1 two-and-three-quarter-ounce bag pork skins
1 jalapeno pepper (1.3-ounce single)
1 packet chili seasoning from Ramen
4 flour tortillas
hot sauce to taste

**Directions**
Dice spam into small pieces and lightly crush pork skins. Add hot water to pork skins bag and carefully knead to hydrate. Dice

up jalapeno pepper and pickle. In a large spread bowl, combine spam, pork skins, jalapeno pepper, pickle, and chili seasoning. Mix well. Coat flour tortillas with squeeze cheese and spoon on mixture, Roll up burritos and place 4 in a rice bag. Heat bag in a hot pot for 2 hours. When cook time is complete, place all 4 in a large spread bowl, and top with hot sauce.

> We are not at our best perched at the summit,
> we are climbers, at our best when the way is steep.
> – J.W. Gardner

# Sweet and Sour-Mexican Style

Contributed by Francisco Villela

### Ingredients
2 jalapeno peppers (1.3-ounce singles)
3 packets sweetener
1½ tablespoons sandwich spread
2½ coffee mugs hot water
1 three-and-a-half-ounce package mackerel
3 tablespoons BBQ sauce
2 three-ounce beef Ramen noodles
1 two-and-three-quarter-ounce bag pork skins
1/2 of a nine-ounce pickle (any flavor)

### Directions
This is a two-step recipe best executed with two hot pots. First step: Dice pickle and jalapeno peppers. Drain juice from mackerel into an insert cup or a rice bag and combine pickle pieces, 1/2 the pickle juice, jalapeno peppers, beef seasoning from Ramen, sweeteners, BBQ sauce, and sandwich spread. Stir well and heat in a hot pot for 30 minutes. Stir occasionally. Now add mackerel and cook an additional 30 minutes. This will be your sauce.

Step two: About 10 minutes before sauce is done, break the Ramen soups into 4 pieces each, place in a large spread bowl with hot water, cover tightly, and cook. When sauce is ready, drain excess water from Ramen and fluff up. Add 3-4 tablespoons hot water to pork skins bag and hydrate by carefully kneading. Pour sauce over noodles and mix well. Top off with pork skins and lightly mix again. Now eat up. This is one meal to truly enjoy

The best general is the one who never fights. – Sun Tzu

# Tex-Mex Tamale

Contributed by Bob Leach

**Ingredients**

1 sixteen-ounce bag corn chips
4½ coffee mugs hot water
1 nine-ounce pickle (any flavor)
2 three-ounce chili Ramen noodles
6 tablespoons salad dressing
1 eleven-and-a-quarter-ounce package chili-no beans
1/4 of an eleven-ounce bag party mix
2 jalapeno peppers (1.3-ounce singles)
1/2 of a 12 oz bag of refried beans, approx. 1½ coffee mugs
1/4 of an eight-ounce bag rice (approximately 1/2 coffee mug)
1/3 of a sixteen-ounce bottle squeeze cheese

**Directions**

Add party mix to corn chips and crush in bag. Add 1/2 of a coffee mug hot water to bag (enough for it to stick together) and knead into a dough. Flatten mixture in bag like a pizza. Wrap in a towel and set aside for 30 minutes. Dice jalapeno peppers and pickle in a large spread bowl and mix-in refried beans, Ramen, rice, and rest of hot water. Cover tightly and cook for 15 minutes. Rinse chili package and heat in a hot pot. When chip mixture is ready, cut down the center of bag to open. Coat dough with salad dressing and cheese, leaving an inch uncovered around edges. On half this area, cover evenly with rice and bean mixture and a little more cheese. Carefully fold and pinch around the edges. Pour hot chili package over top for a great side dish to a hearty meal.

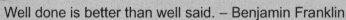

Well done is better than well said. – Benjamin Franklin

# TNT's Tamales

Contributed by Troy Traylor

## Ingredients

1 eight-ounce package Mexican beef
1 sixteen-ounce bag corn chips
1 packet chicken seasoning from Ramen
1/3 coffee mug hot water
1 two-and-three-quarter-ounce bag pork skins
1 two-ounce package cream cheese*
salsa to taste

## Directions

Rinse off meat package and heat in a hot pot. While this is heating, crush corn chips into a fine powder, in the chip bag. Add the chicken seasoning to bag and shake well. Add a little less than 1/4 coffee mug hot water to bag and knead into dough. Once kneaded, flatten out evenly in the chip bag. Cut bag open length wise to air dry for 30 minutes. During this time, lightly crush pork skins in their bag. Add 3 tablespoons hot water to this bag and knead to hydrate. When meat package is hot, combine beef, pork skins, and cream cheese in a spread bowl and mix well. Now cut dough into 4 pieces. Top each piece with beef mixture. Roll up dough around mixture and seal. Place your 4 tamales in a rice bag and heat in a hot pot for 2 hours. Once cook time is complete, place all 4 in a spread bowl and top with salsa. Not quite like mom makes, but close.

*Package of cream cheese will be equal to 4 tablespoons.

> Know thy work and do it.
> – Thomas Carlyle

# Tortilla Bowls

Contributed by Chris Killman

## Ingredients

1 eleven-and-a-quarter-ounce package chili no beans
1 five-ounce summer sausage
2 coffee mugs hot water
3 tablespoons butter
2 jalapeno peppers (1.3-ounce singles)
1 eight-ounce bag instant rice
8 flour tortillas
1 tablespoon onion powder
salt, black pepper, and squeeze cheese to taste

## Directions

Rinse off chili package and heat in a hot pot. Dice the jalapeno peppers and summer sausage and set aside. In a large spread bowl, combine rice and hot water. Cover tightly to cook for 10 minutes. Poke holes throughout tortillas. Heat tortillas in a paper towel lined microwave for 10 seconds on high. Evenly spread 4 tortillas in each of two bowls. Heat each bowl on high for one minute. Rotate each bowl 60° twice, heating for an additional 30 seconds each time. Your tortillas should now feel hard like a cracker. Set these bowls aside and using a separate spread bowl combine the jalapeno peppers and summer sausage. Cover with a towel and heat on high in a microwave for 2-3 minutes. Remove bowl from microwave and add rice, butter, salt, pepper, onion powder, chili package, and summer sausage. Mix well. Divide this mixture between the two-tortilla bowls and top with cheese.

> It takes less work to succeed than to fail.
> – W. Clement Stone

# Tri-Fecta Burritos

Contributed by Troy Traylor

### Ingredients
1 five-ounce summer sausage
1 seven-ounce package chicken chunks
1 coffee mug refried beans
1½ coffee mugs hot water
2 jalapeno peppers (1.3-ounce singles)
1 two-and-three-quarter-ounce bag pork skins
1 package chicken seasoning from Ramen
4 flour tortillas
squeeze cheese to taste

### Directions
Dice up summer sausage into small pieces. Drain and shred chicken chunks. Combine refried beans and hot water in a large spread bowl, stir, cover tightly, and cook for 10-12 minutes. While waiting, dice jalapeno peppers and lightly crush pork skins. Once beans are ready, combine all ingredients and mix well. Spoon the mixture onto tortillas and roll or fold. There you have it – three flavors and one great taste.

Resolve says, "I will." The man says,
"I will climb this mountain. They told me it is
too high, too far, too steep, too rocky
and too difficult. But it's my mountain.
I will climb it. You will see me waving from
the top or dead on the side from trying."
– Jim Rohn

# Special Days for the Foodie

October
(1st): National Pumpkin Spice Day, World Vegetarian Day
(2nd): World Farm Animals Day
(3rd): National Soft Taco Day
(4th): National Taco Day
(5th): National Apple Betty Day, Rocky Mountain Oyster Day
(6th): National Noodle Day
(7th): National Frappe Day
(8th): National Fluffernutter Day
(9th): National Pizza and Beer Day, National Hoagie Day
(10th): National Tic Tac Day, National Angel Food Cake Day
(11th): National Sausage Pizza Day
(12th): National Gumbo Day, Pumpkin Pie Day
(13th): Yorkshire Pudding Day, National M & M Day
(14th): National Dessert Day
(15th): National Mushroom Day, National Red Wine Day
(16th): National Liqueur Day, National World Food Day
(17th): National Pasta Day
(18th): National Chocolate Cupcake Day
(19th): National Seafood Bisque Day
(20th): National Brandied Fruit Day
(21st): National Pumpkin Cheesecake Day
(22nd): National Nut Day
(23rd): National Boston Cream Pie Day
(24th): National Bologna Day, Feast of Good & Plenty
(25th): National Greasy Foods Day
(26th): National Mincemeat Day, National Pumpkin Day
(27th): National Potato Day, American Beer Day
(28th): National Chocolate Day
(29th): National Oatmeal Day
(30th): National Candy Corn Day
(31st): National Caramel Apple Day

# Section VIII:
# Cakes and Pies of All Kinds

# Cool History of Cakes

The word "cake" is known to have its origins in the Viking culture, from the Old Norse "kaka." Old Norse had a marked influence on Old English, propelling the language towards Middle English, from which the oldest known written documentation of the word "cake" is noted. (If you are familiar with Shakespeare, his writing still has some remnants of Middle English.)

As you can imagine, cakes diverged from the broader category of bread, taking on its own techniques of baking and eating patterns. When thinking about the distinction between bread and cake, it can be tough to draw a clear line. According to the online Oxford Dictionary, a cake is "a baked mass of bread or substance of
similar kind, distinguished from a loaf or other ordinary bread, either by its form or by its composition." What form or composition makes a cake distinguishable from bread?

Molds for cakes such as cake hoops or pans have been used since at least the mid-17th century. Geoffrey Chaucer, known as the father of English literature (author of the famous book *The Canterbury Tales*), wrote about immense cakes that served special occasions in the 14th century. One cake was made with 13 kg (or over 28 lbs.) of flour! Fast forward to the 19th century, cake baking adapted bicarbonate, a chemical raising agent, and baking powder, replacing yeast and providing leavening power with less effort. And in the early-to-mid-20th century, the ability to bake a good cake was a prized skill among housewives.

# Some Cool Facts on Peanut Butter

– Peanuts are actually not a nut, but legumes grown underground.

– The U.S. is the third largest producer of peanuts (thanks to Georgia and Texas). China and India are first and second, respectively.

– More than half of the American peanut crop goes into making peanut butter.

– U.S. presidents Jimmy Carter and Thomas Jefferson were peanut farmers.

– It takes about 540 peanuts to make a 12 oz. jar of peanut butter.

– Americans eat around 700 million pounds of peanut butter per year, about 3 pounds per person.

– The average American child eats 1500 PB and J sandwiches before graduating from high school.

# Banana Cake

Contributed by Troy Traylor

### Ingredients
1 sixteen-ounce package vanilla crème cookies
5 tablespoons hot water
3 bananas
1 two-ounce package energy mix
4 tablespoons peanut butter

### Directions
Separate crème from cookies and place crème aside. Crush all cookies into a fine powder and place in a large spread bowl. Add 4 tablespoons hot water (you want it just moist enough to stick together) and knead into a pliable dough. Dice bananas and add to mixture. Knead again to mix all thoroughly. Flatten out mixture into the bottom of the spread bowl evenly. Sprinkle the energy mix over top of cake and use a spoon to lightly press all into top of cake. Place bowl under a fan to dry for 1 hour. While waiting, combine crème from cookies, peanut butter, and 1 tablespoon hot water in an insert cup and place in a hot pot, un-stirred, for 30 minutes. Remove from hot pot, stir well, and place back in hot pot for an additional 30 minutes. When dry time is complete, remove insert from hot pot, stir well, and pour over cake. Even out and place bowl back under a fan for 1 more hour. This is soooo good!

> "
> The most important single ingredient in the formula of success is knowing how to get along with people.
> – Theodore Roosevelt
> "

# Brownie Cake

Contributed by Troy Traylor

## Ingredients
4 slices white bread (no crust)
1 sixteen-ounce box honey buns
1 ten-ounce bag hot chocolate mix
3/4 coffee mug regular oatmeal
2 packages M and M's
1/4 coffee mug hot water
2 snicker's bars

## Directions
Take crust off of bread and dice honey buns into small pieces. Set snicker's bars aside and combine all remaining ingredients in a large spread bowl. Use two spoons and mix well. This will be a very stiff mixture. Flatten out mixture into the bottom of the spread bowl and even out. Place bowl under a fan to dry for 3-4 hours. This will stiffen up. About 30 minutes before dry time is complete, place both snicker's bars in a hot pot to melt (leave in wrapper). After mixture is dry, remove snickers from hot pot and spread evenly over cake. Place bowl back under a fan for 2 more hours so it cools and sets up. Cut and serve. What a treat this is.

*If you cannot get a box of honey buns, use 3 large ones instead.

* A 10-ounce bag of hot chocolate mix is equal to just shy of a 12-ounce coffee mug.

Success is a journey not a destination.
– Paula Scaletta

# Chocolate Covered Cherry Vanilla Pie

Contributed by Ernest Riley

### Ingredients
1 sixteen-ounce bag vanilla wafers
2 tablespoons butter
2 four-ounce packages instant milk
2 packages sweetener
1/4 of a twelve-ounce Sprite
6 individual oatmeal crème pies
4½ tablespoons hot water
2 packets of cherry Kool Aid (.14 ounce)
8 tablespoons vanilla cappuccino
1 Hershey's bar

### Directions
Crush vanilla wafers into a fine powder, mush oatmeal crème pies and combine in a large spread bowl with butter and hot water and knead into pliable dough. Add water a little at a time, making sure the dough does not become too wet. Evenly flatten mixture out into the bottom of the spread bowl. Starting in the center, using your knuckles, press down firmly and work your way around bowl, towards the outside. Dough will begin to climb sides of bowl. Work this into your pie crust and smooth out when done. You want dough about 3/4 way up sides of bowl. This is your crust. Place this bowl under a fan to dry for 1 hour. About 15 minutes before dry, using a separate spread bowl, combine all remaining ingredients, except Hershey's bar. Use two spoons and whip until mixture is smooth and creamy. Do not leave any lumps or clumps. Best to start with a little Sprite at a time. Mixture should be thick like pancake batter. Once all is whipped, pour into pie crust and

smooth out. Place bowl under a fan to dry. While drying, place Hershey's bar in a hot pot to fully melt. About one hour into dry time, drizzle Hershey's bar allover top of pie. Allow this to now dry for 2-3 hours. Yummy!

*Packages of Kool Aid are equal to 2 tablespoons each.

*Packages of sweetener are equal to 2 tablespoons each.

We are builders of our characters. We have different positions, spheres, capacities, privileges, different work to do in the world, different temporal fabrics to raise; but we are all alike in this – all are architects of fate.
– John Fothergill Waterhouse Ware

# Chocolate Peanut Butter Cake

Contributed by Robert McKinney

**Ingredients**
1 thirteen-ounce box graham crackers
3 tablespoons hot water
2 Hershey's Bars
1/3 jar peanut butter
2 one-ounce chick-o-sticks

**Directions**
Crush the graham crackers and place all in a large spread bowl. Add the hot water, just enough to stick, and knead into a pliable dough. Evenly flatten mixture into the bottom of the spread bowl and place under a fan to dry for 1 hour. While waiting, dice the Hershey's bars into small pieces and put in your hot pot lid. Fill up hot pot and place lid upside down on pot so chocolate melts. Set jar of peanut butter in a separate bowl, filled with hot water so it too can soften. When dry time is up for cake, cover cake with half
the peanut butter and drizzle half the Hershey's bars over top. Now repeat with the other half of peanut butter and Hershey's bars. Crush up the chick-o-sticks and sprinkle over cake. Place bowl back under a fan to dry for 2 hours. All will set up nicely.

> If a man empties his purse into his head,
> no man can take it away from him.
> An investment in knowledge always pays the best interest.
> – Benjamin Franklin

# Commissary Concoction

Contributed by Troy Traylor

**Ingredients**
1 sixteen-ounce package Duplex crème cookies
3½ packages maple syrup*
1/2 coffee mug hot chocolate mix
2 packages nutty bars
1 two-ounce package salted peanuts
1 package apple cinnamon oatmeal* (43 grams)
1 package regular oatmeal* (43 grams)
2 one-ounce chick-o-sticks

**Directions**
Separate crème from cookies. Crush cookies into a fine powder and set crème aside. Place all in a large spread bowl, along with 1½ packages maple syrup, and knead into pliable dough. You want this just moist enough, so it all sticks together. If the mixture is still a little dry, add a few drops of syrup at a time until moist. Starting in the center, using your knuckles, press down firmly and work your way around the bowl, towards the outside. Dough will begin to climb sides of bowl. Work this into your pie crust. Smooth out when done. Crust should be about 2 inches from top of bowl. Place bowl under a fan to dry for 2 hours. While waiting, in a second large spread bowl, combine hot chocolate mix with 1½ packages of maple syrup and stir until well mixed. Lightly crush nutty bars and add to hot chocolate mixture, along with regular oatmeal and salted peanuts. Mix this well. Mixture will be very thick. Flatten out mixture in bowl and sit with other bowl to dry a bit. While it is drying, place crème from cookies in an insert cup with remaining 1/2 package of syrup. Do not stir just yet. Allow this to heat for 30 minutes then whip.

Place back in hot pot for another 30 minutes. Stir occasionally. When crust is dry, use your ID card and run around inside of hot chocolate bowl. Turn bowl upside down and work mixture out. Set this inside pie crust, press down firmly, and even out. Sprinkle apple cinnamon oatmeal over top and use a spoon to press oatmeal into pie. Whip icing and pour over top of this. Crush chick-o-sticks and sprinkle evenly. Place bowl back under a fan for 1 hour before you cut. Icing will stiffen.

*Packages of maple syrup are equal to 3 tablespoons each.
*Packages of oatmeal are equal to a 1/4 coffee mug each.

> Abuse no one and no living thing, for abuse turns the wise
> ones to fools and robs the spirit of its vision ...
> When it comes your time to die, do not be like those
> whose hearts are filled with fear of death, so that when
> their time comes, they weep and pray for a little more
> time to live their lives over again in a different way.
> Sing your death song like a hero coming home.
> – Tecumseh, Shawnee, 1768-1813

# Commissary Concoction II

Contributed by Troy Traylor

**Ingredients**
1 sixteen-ounce package Duplex cookies
5½ packages maple syrup*
1/2 coffee mug hot chocolate mix
1 four-ounce package instant milk*
1/2 of a two-ounce package cream cheese
1 one-ounce chick-o-stick

**Directions**
This recipe takes a little time, but the results are outstanding. To begin, separate crème from cookies. Crush cookies into a fine powder and set crème aside. Place all in a large spread bowl, along with 1½ packages maple syrup, and knead into pliable dough. You want this just moist enough, so it all sticks together. If the mixture is still a little dry, add a few drops of syrup at a time until moist. Starting in the center, using your knuckles, press down firmly and work your way around the bowl, towards the outside. Dough will begin to climb sides of bowl. Work this into your pie crust. Smooth out when done. Place bowl under a fan to dry for 2 hours. While waiting, in a second large spread bowl, combine hot chocolate mix with 1½ packages of maple syrup and stir until well mixed. This mixture will be very thick. Leave as is in the bowl until crust is ready. Now, using a separate bowl, combine the crème from the cookies, instant milk, cream cheese, and 3 packages maple syrup and whip well. Want all lumps and clumps gone. May need to add a 1/2 tablespoon water as you whip. You will want this mixture a little thicker than pancake batter. Once whipped, put hot chocolate mixture inside the crust and even out. Press down firmly on this.

Now pour milk mixture over this and even out. Crush chick-o-stick and sprinkle over top of this pie. Allow this to dry under a fan for 3-4 hours. Mixture will thicken up. Words cannot describe how good this is.

*Packages of maple syrup are equal to 3 tablespoons each.
*Package of milk is equal to 2/3 of a 12-ounce coffee mug.
*Packages of cream cheese is equal to 4 tablespoons each.

I've learned that people will forget what you said, people will forget what you did, but people will never forget how you made them feel
– Maya Angelou, civil rights activist

# Cookie Cake

Contributed by Thomas Hall

**Ingredients**

1 sixteen-ounce package Duplex crème cookies
2 tablespoons peanut butter
2 two-ounce packages salted peanuts
5 tablespoons hot water
3 tablespoons French vanilla creamer
1 regular size Milky Way
1 one-ounce chick-o-stick

**Directions**

Separate crème from cookies, crush cookies into a fine powder and set crème aside. In a large spread bowl mix cookie powder, peanut butter, peanuts, and 4 tablespoons hot water and knead into pliable dough. Do not make too wet, just a moist consistency. Evenly flatten dough in bowl. Place bowl under a fan to dry for 1½ hours. While waiting, combine French vanilla, crème from cookies, and 1 tablespoon hot water in an insert cup. Now dice candy bar into small pieces and add to insert. Do not stir just yet. Place insert into a hot pot to heat for 30 minutes. Now remove insert and stir well. Place insert back into hot pot to heat until cake is dry. Remove insert from hot pot, stir well, and pour over cake. Smooth out. Crush chick-o-stick and sprinkle over cake. Now allow cake to dry under a fan for 1-2 hours. Icing will stiffen up.

He that cannot obey, cannot command.
– Benjamin Franklin

# Crazy Cookie Cake

Contributed by Troy Traylor

### Ingredients
1 sixteen-ounce package Duplex crème cookies
3 one-ounce chick-o-sticks
2 packages maple syrup*
1 tablespoon hot water
1 package maple brown sugar oatmeal* (43 grams)
1/2 coffee mug raisins
1/2 tablespoon peanut butter

### Directions
Separate crème from cookies and set crème aside. Crush all cookies into a fine powder and place into a large spread bowl. Some chunks are okay. Lightly crush chick-o-sticks. Add chick-o-sticks, raisins, and syrup to bowl and knead into pliable dough. You only want moist enough to stick together. Flatten dough out into the bottom of the spread bowl and even out. Place this bowl under a fan to dry for 1 hour. While waiting, place crème from cookies and 1 tablespoon hot water in an insert cup and place in a hot pot. Do not whip or stir just yet. Allow to heat 30 minutes then whip well. Place back in hot pot for an additional 30 minutes. When dry time is up, remove insert cup from hot pot, stir in peanut butter, and pour over cake. Even out and let dry for another 30-45 minutes before you cut. Makes 8 wonderful pieces. Invite an associate or two to join you.

*Package of oatmeal is equal to a 1/4 coffee mug.

> One thought fills immensity.
> – William Blake

# Orange Ya-Glad Cake

Contributed by Troy Traylor

**Ingredients**

1 sixteen-ounce package vanilla crème cookies
2 ten-and-a-quarter-ounce bags orange slices
4 packages apple cinnamon oatmeal (.43 grams)
8 tablespoons hot water
1/4 of a four-ounce package instant milk
2 packages orange electrolyte* (.34 ounce)
2 tablespoons butter
2 packages sweetener

**Directions**

Separate crème from cookies and set aside. Crush cookies, chunks are okay for this one. Dice orange slices into small pieces. Using a large spread bowl, combine cookies, 2/3 orange slices, 2 packages oatmeal, and 7 tablespoons hot water. Knead thoroughly. Now add the remaining 2 oatmeal packs to mixture and knead again. You want this just moist enough to stick together without falling apart. Maintain a moist consistency, even if you need to add more water. Evenly flatten  out dough into the bottom of the spread bowl. Place bowl under a fan to dry for 1 hour. While drying, in an insert cup or a rice bag, combine crème from cookies, instant milk, both electrolytes, butter, and sweeteners. Place in a hot pot to cook. No water is needed. Stir occasionally to a thick consistency. When cake is dry, remove insert cup from hot pot, whip well, and pour over cake. Should even itself out. Decorate cake with remaining orange slices. Place bowl back under a fan to dry for another 2-3 hours. Orange ya glad you made this one?

*Packages of electrolyte are equal to 1 tablespoon electrolyte or 4 tablespoons Kool Aid.
*Packages of sweetener are equal to 2 tablespoons each.

Men best show their character in trifles, where they are not on their guard. It is in the simplest habits, that we often see the boundless egotism which pays no regard to the feelings of others and denies nothing to itself.
– Arthur Schopenhauer

# Pineapple Delight

Contributed by Paul Scoles

### Ingredients
1 sixteen-ounce package vanilla crème cookies
1½ servings pineapples (four-ounces)
1/2 coffee mug raisins
1/2 of a .34-ounce packet of lemon lime electrolyte*
water will vary

### Directions
Separate crème from cookies and set crème aside. Crush all cookies into a fine powder and place all in a large spread bowl. Add pineapples, half of the half packet of electrolyte, and raisins to bowl and knead thoroughly. I mean thoroughly! The pineapples carry a lot of juice so water will be little, if any. You only want this moist enough to stick together. If any water is added it is best to go a half tablespoon at a time. If you get the cake too wet just add a package of regular oatmeal (1/4 coffee mug). This will absorb moisture. Once kneaded, evenly flatten out into the bottom of the spread bowl. Place bowl under a fan to dry for 1 hour. While waiting place crème from cookies, the remaining electrolyte, and 1 tablespoon water in an insert cup. Do not stir or whip this until after it heats for 30 minutes. Remove from hot pot, whip, and place back in hot pot for an additional 30 minutes. When dry time is up, remove insert from hot pot, whip, and pour over cake. Even out and wait 30-45 minutes before you cut for icing to set up.

*Package of electrolyte is equal to 1 tablespoon electrolyte or 4 tablespoons Kool Aid.

It is better to be faithful than famous. – Teddy Roosevelt

# Pineapple Delight II

Contributed by Paul Scoles

**Ingredients**
1 sixteen-ounce package vanilla crème cookies
1½ servings pineapples (four-ounces)
1/2 coffee mug raisins
1/2 of a .34-ounce packet lemon lime electrolyte*
1 two-ounce package salted peanuts
1 package strawberry and cream oatmeal (.43 grams)
1 package regular oatmeal (.43 grams)
1/2 coffee mug hot chocolate mix
water will vary

**Directions**
Separate crème from cookies and set crème aside. Crush cookies into a fine powder and place in a large spread bowl. Now add the pineapples, raisins, half of the half packet of electrolyte, peanuts, and strawberry and cream oatmeal to bowl and knead thoroughly. Pineapples carry a lot of juice so water will vary, if any. You want this to be moist only. Once you have this mixed into pliable dough, add the hot chocolate mix to bowl and knead again. Now you may need to add a tablespoon of water. Mixture will be very thick. Now evenly flatten this out into the bottom of the spread bowl. Place bowl under a fan to dry for 1 hour. While waiting, place crème from cookies in an insert cup with the remaining electrolyte and 1 tablespoon water. After heating for 30 minutes, whip well and place back in hot pot for an additional 30 minutes. When dry time is complete, spread the regular oatmeal over cake evenly and use your spoon to press into top of cake. Now remove insert cup from hot pot, whip, and pour this over cake and even out. Place bowl back under a fan

for another 30-45 minutes. Icing will set up. Cut and serve. The regular oatmeal will help icing stick to cake. Hot chocolate does not allow icing to stick sometimes.

*Package of electrolyte is equal to 1 tablespoon electrolyte or 4 tablespoons Kool Aid.
*Packages of oatmeal are equal to 1/4 coffee mug each

The need to be right all the time is the biggest bar to new ideas. It is better to have enough ideas for some of them to be wrong than to always be right by having no ideas at all.
– Edward DeBono

# Sewin Oats Cake

Contributed by Troy Traylor

### Ingredients
1 ten-package box of instant oatmeal
2 handfuls raisins
3 two-ounce packages salted peanuts
4 packages maple syrup
2 tablespoons peanut butter
1/4 coffee mug hot chocolate mix
2 tablespoons hot water

### Directions
Combine all oatmeal, raisins, peanuts, and syrup in a large spread bowl and knead very well. Evenly flatten in bottom of spread bowl. Place bowl under a fan and let set up while you prepare the icing. Combine peanut butter, hot chocolate mix, and water in an insert cup. Do not stir just yet. Place insert cup in a hot pot and heat for 30 minutes before you stir. Place back in a hot pot for an additional 30 minutes. Remove insert from hot pot, whip well, and spread evenly over cake. Allow to dry for 1 hour before you cut. Nice and healthy cake.

*Packages of syrup are equal to 3 tablespoons each.

Without an acquaintance with the rules of propriety, it is impossible for the character to be established.
– Confucius (551 BC-479 BC), *The Confucian Analects*

# Simple Cake

Contributed by Darrell Pickett

## Ingredients

1 sixteen-ounce package vanilla crème cookies
4-5 tablespoons hot water
1 tablespoon peanut butter
1 package M & M's
1 one-ounce chick-o-stick

## Directions

Separate crème from cookies and set crème aside. Crush cookies into a fine powder and put all in a large spread bowl. Add 4 tablespoons water to this bowl and knead into pliable dough, just moist enough so it all sticks together. Once kneaded, evenly flatten out dough in bowl. Place bowl under a fan to dry for 1 hour. About 30 minutes before dry time is up, put the crème from the cookies into an insert cup and add peanut butter and 1 tablespoon of water. After heating for 20 minutes in a hot pot, stir well and
place back in a hot pot for 10-15 minutes more. When dry time is complete, remove insert from hot pot, stir well, and pour over cake. Decorate cake with M & M's. Now crush up chick-o-stick and sprinkle over top. Place bowl back under a fan for 1 more hour. See how good the simple things in life can be.

*Quantum mutatus ab illo*
How changed from what he once was
– Virgil

# Soul Reviver

Contributed by Joseph Garcia

### Ingredients

1 sixteen-ounce package Duplex crème cookies
2 packages Maria cookies (11.2 ounces total)
3 oatmeal crème pies
1 tablespoon cappuccino (any flavor)
1 heaping tablespoon peanut butter
1 package nutty bars
1 package maple brown sugar oatmeal (.43 grams)
1 package apple cinnamon oatmeal (.43 grams)
1 package maple syrup
1 package M & M's
10 tablespoons hot water

### Directions

Separate crème from cookies and set crème aside. Crush cookies in a large spread bowl. Add 7 tablespoons water, maple brown sugar oatmeal, and oatmeal crème pies to bowl and mix well. Get mixture just moist enough to stick together. Evenly flatten out mixture into bottom of spread bowl. Dry under fan for 3 hours. After 2½ hours, in an insert cup, combine crème from cookies, peanut butter, cappuccino, and 2 tablespoons hot water, and whip well. Heat insert in hot pot for 30 minutes, stirring occasionally. Remove insert from hot pot, whip icing and evenly pour over cake. Drizzle syrup over icing and sprinkle oatmeal over that. Decorate with crushed M & M's and nutty bar. Allow icing to sit for 1 hour before you cut cake. This is a Soul Reviver for real!

If you add value out, you'll bring value in.
– Jeffrey Gitomer

# State Cake

Contributed by Troy Traylor

### Ingredients
1 sixteen-ounce package Duplex crème cookies
1 sixteen-ounce box honey buns*
1 tablespoon instant coffee
1/4 coffee mug French vanilla cappuccino
3 packages maple syrup*
1 tablespoon hot water

### Directions
Separate crème from cookies and set crème aside. Crush all cookies into a fine powder and place in a large spread bowl. Dice all honey buns into fairly small pieces. Place these in with cookie crumbs, along with the coffee and cappuccino. Toss a little. Now add the maple syrup and knead all into pliable dough. Evenly flatten out dough into the bottom of the spread bowl. Dry under a fan for 1 hour. While waiting, combine crème from cookies and the water in an insert cup. Place cup in a hot pot un-stirred for 30 minutes. Whip well after 30 minutes and place back in hot pot for an
additional 30 minutes. When cake is dry, remove insert cup from hot pot, whip well. and pour over cake. Smooth out and place back under a fan for 1 hour before you cut.

*If you cannot get a box of honey buns just use 3 large honey buns.
*Packages of maple syrup are equal to 3 tablespoons each,

Language is the dress of thought.
– Samuel Johnson (1709-1784)

# Sweet Cookie Cake

Contributed by Michelle Vargas

**Ingredients**
1 sixteen-ounce package Duplex crème cookies
1 package maple brown sugar oatmeal* (43 grams)
8 tablespoons hot water
2 tablespoons peanut butter
5 tablespoons hot chocolate mix

**Directions**
Separate crème from cookies and set crème aside. Crush cookies into a fine powder. Some chunks are ok. Place all in a large spread bowl with the oatmeal and 5½ tablespoons hot water. Knead into pliable dough, just moist enough to stick together. If you need more water only add a 1/2 tablespoon at a time. Evenly flatten dough into the bottom of the spread bowl and place under a fan to dry for 1 hour. While waiting, combine crème from cookies and 1 tablespoon hot water in an insert cup. After heating in a hot pot for 30 minutes, whip well and place back in a hot pot for an additional 30 minutes. When cake is dry, add the peanut butter and hot chocolate mix to insert and whip until all dissolves. Pour this over cake and even out. Allow to dry for another 30-45 minutes before you cut cake. Icing will stiffen up.

*Package of oatmeal is equal to a 1/4 coffee mug.

The louder he talked of his honor,
the faster we counted our spoons.
– Ralph Waldo Emerson (1803-1882)

# Sweet Jesus

Contributed by Troy Traylor

## Ingredients

1 sixteen-ounce package Duplex cookies
4 packages maple syrup
1 heaping handful raisins
1 tablespoon hot water
1/2 coffee mug hot chocolate mix
1 two-ounce package salted peanuts
3 tablespoons peanut butter
1 package regular oatmeal (.43 ounce)

## Directions

Separate crème from cookies and set crème aside. In one large spread bowl, crush 2 rows plus 4 cookies (26 cookies) into a fine powder. In a second spread bowl, crush the remaining cookies and add the hot chocolate mix. In bowl #1, add 1¾ packages maple syrup and knead into pliable dough. Flatten dough then using your knuckles, starting in the center, press down firmly and work the dough into a pie crust with about a 2-inch lip. Dry under a fan for 1-2 hours. In bowl #2, add peanuts, raisins, and 1¼ packages maple syrup and mix well. Set this with bowl #1 to dry. Once dry, coat pie crust with peanut butter and hot chocolate mixture. Use a spoon and even out and press. Set aside for a few more minutes. In an insert cup, combine crème from cookies and hot water. Melt in an insert cup in a hot pot for 30 minutes, stirring occasionally. Pour this over the pie and smooth out. Allow to sit for 1 hour before you cut. So good you will sing praises.

When there's no Law, there's no Bread.
– Benjamin Franklin

# The Whole Caboodle Cake

Contributed by Troy Traylor

## Ingredients
1 sixteen-ounce package Duplex crème cookies
1 sixteen-ounce box oatmeal crème pies
1/2 coffee mug hot chocolate mix
1/2 coffee mug raisins
4 tablespoons peanut butter
1 two-ounce package salted peanuts
4½ tablespoons hot water

## Directions
Separate crème from cookies and set crème aside. Crush cookies slightly, leaving some chunks. Take an ID card and separate oatmeal crème pies. Cover a large spread bowl with these, forming a pie crust with the crème side up. Leave no gaps. In a separate bowl, knead together hot chocolate mix, cookie pieces, and 3½ tablespoons hot water. Once this is kneaded add 3 tablespoons peanut butter and knead again to a very thick and firm mixture. Take your peanuts and raisins and work into this mixture until evenly distributed. Place this mixture inside pie crust, press firmly, and dry under a fan for 1 hour. Now combine crème from cookies, remaining peanut butter, and 1 tablespoon hot water. Place insert in hot pot for 30 minutes before you whip, then allow it to heat another 30 minutes. After cake is dry, remove insert from hot pot, stir, and spread over cake evenly. Allow icing to set up for 30-45 minutes before you cut. Makes 8 big boy slices.

Patience is the companion of wisdom.
– St. Augustine

# Special Days for the Foodie

November

(1st): National Bison Day, National Pâté Day

(2nd): National Deviled Egg Day

(3rd): National Sandwich Day

(4th): National Candy Day

(5th): National Doughnut Day, National Chinese Take-out Day

(6th): National Nachos Day

(7th): National Bittersweet Chocolate with Almonds Day

(8th): National Cappuccino Day

(9th): National Greek Yogurt Day

(10th): National Vanilla Cupcake Day

(11th): National Sundae Day

(12th): National Pizza with the Works Except Anchovies Day

(13th): National Indian Pudding Day, Feast of St. Diego Alacala

(14th): National Pickle 'Appreciation' Day

(15th): National Raisin Bran Cereal Day

(16th): National Fast Food Day

(17th): National Baklava Day, Homemade Bread Day

(18th): National Apple Cider Day, National Vichyssoise Day

(19th): National Macchiato Day

(20th): National Peanut Butter Fudge Day

(21st): National Cranberry Day, National Gingerbread Cookie Day

(22nd): National Cranberry Relish Day, National Cashew Day

(23rd): National Espresso Day

(24th): National Sardines Day

(25th): National Parfait Day, National "Eat with a Friend" Day

(26th): National Cake Day

(27th): National Bavarian Cream Pie Day

(28th): National French Toast Day

(29th): National Chocolates Day, National Lemon Creme Pie Day

(30th): National Mousse Day

December
(1st): National Fried Pie Day
(2nd): National Fritters Day, Feast of St. Bibiana
(3nd): National Peppermint Latte Day
(4th): National Cookie Day
(5th): National Comfort Food Day, Repeal of Prohibition Day
(6th): National Gazpacho Day, National Microwave Oven Day
(7th): National Cotton Candy Day, Ferry Floss Day(Great Britain)
(8th): National Brownie Day
(9th): National Pastry Day
(10th): National Lager Day
(11th): National "Have a Bagel" Day
(12th): National Cocoa Day, National Ambrosia Day
(13th): National Popcorn String Day
(14th): National Biscuits and Gravy Day
(15th): National Lemon Cupcake Day
(16th): National Chocolate Covered Anything Day
(17th): National Maple Syrup Day
(18th): National "I Love Honey" Day
(19th): National Hard Candy Day, National Oatmeal Muffin Day
(20th): National Sangria Day
(21st): National French Fried Shrimp Day
(22nd): National Date Nut Bread Day
(23rd): National Bake Day
(24th): National Egg Nog Day
(25th): National Pumpkin Pie Day, National "Kiss the Cook" Day
(26th): National Candy Cane Day
(27th): National Fruitcake Day
(28th): National Box of Chocolates Day
(29th): National "Get on the Scales" Day
(30th): National Bacon Day, Baking Soda Day
(31st): National Champagne Day, National Vinegar Day

# Section IX:
# A Few Cheesecakes

# Some Cool History on Cheesecakes

Cheesecakes were quite popular amongst the Greek. Physical anthropologists excavated cheese molds on the Greek islands of Samos, which were dated circa 2000 B.C., but cheese most likely existed way earlier possibly into prehistory (the period in human history before the invention of writing). We know, however, that cheesecakes were served to athletes during the first Olympic Games held in 776 B.C. on the Isle of Delos under the belief that these cakes were a good source of energy. Unlike today's modern cheesecakes, these ancient cheesecakes had very simple Ingredients: flour, wheat, honey, and cheese. Back in the day, cheese curds were made in animal stomachs or skin, which would make the food safety people of today cringe. Supposedly, they were also served as wedding cakes. I imagine these cheesecakes to somewhat resemble today's pancakes.

Cheese has ancient origins and an even more mysterious past. No one knows where it originated, but according to Pliny the Elder, a writer during the Roman Empire, cheese became a sophisticated enterprise, so much that valued foreign cheeses were transported to Rome for the elites there.

It was not until the 18th century, however, that cheesecakes would start to look like something we recognize in the United States today. Around this time, Europeans began to use beaten eggs instead of yeast to make their breads and cakes rise. Removing the overpowering yeast flavor makes cheesecakes taste more like a dessert treat. When Europeans immigrated to America, some brought their cheesecake recipes along.

Cream cheese was an American addition to the cake, and it has since become a staple ingredient in the United States. In 1872, a New York dairy farmer was attempting to replicate the French cheese Neufchatel. Instead, he accidentally discovered a process that resulted in the creation of cream cheese. Three years later, cream cheese was packaged in foil and distributed to local stores under the Philadelphia Cream Cheese brand. The

Philadelphia Cream Cheese brand was purchased in 1903 by the Phoenix Cheese Company, and then it was purchased in 1928 by the Kraft Cheese Company. Kraft continues to make this very same delicious Philadelphia Cream Cheese that we are all familiar with today.

*New York Style Cheesecake*

Of course, no story of cheesecake is complete without delving into the origins of the New York style cheesecake. The Classic New York style cheesecake is served with just the cake – no fruit, chocolate, or caramel is served on the top or the side. This famously smooth-tasting cake gets its signature flavor from extra egg yolks in the cream cheese cake mix.

By the 1900s, New Yorkers were in love with this dessert. Virtually every restaurant had its own version of cheesecake on the menu. New Yorkers have vied for bragging rights for having the original recipe ever since. Even though he is best known for his signature sandwiches, Arnold Reuben (1883-1970) is generally credited for creating the New York Style cheesecake. Reuben was born in Germany and he came to America when he was young. The story goes that Reuben was invited to a dinner party where the hostess served a cherry pie. Allegedly, he was so intrigued by this dish that he experimented with this recipe until he came up with the beloved NY Style cheesecake.

*More Variations in America*

New York is not the only place in America that puts its own spin on cheesecakes. In Chicago, sour cream is added to the recipe to keep it creamy. Meanwhile, Philadelphia cheesecake is known for being lighter and creamier than New York style cheesecake and it can be served with fruit or chocolate toppings. In St. Louis, they enjoy a gooey butter cake, which has an additional layer of cake topping on the cheesecake filling.

*Cheesecake around the World*

Each region of the world also has its own take on the best way to make the dessert. Italians use ricotta cheese, while the

Greeks use mizithra or feta. Germans prefer cottage cheese, while the Japanese use a combination of cornstarch and egg whites. There are specialty cheesecakes that include blue cheese, seafood, spicy chilies, and even tofu! Despite all the variations, the popular dessert's main ingredients – cheese, wheat, and a sweetener – remain the same.

A "doily" is a small ornamental mat made of lace or paper with a lace pattern, typically placed on a plate under a cake or other sweet foods. Can you find the word "DOILY" in this diagram 26 times? Its letters read in a straight line forward, backward, up, down, and diagonally. Good luck!

```
D Y D L D D Y Y D Y Y I
O L D O Y L O L O Y L Y
I Y I O I D O I I D I L
L L D O I L Y O L O O Y
Y D D O I L Y D Y Y D L
D O I L Y D Y L I O D I
D I I D O L L L I L D O
O L O I I L I I I O O D
I Y L O I O O O I O D O
L Y D I O O D L D O D Y
Y L I O D D Y Y L I O D
```

# Chocolate Covered Banana Cheesecake

Contributed by Troy Traylor

### Ingredients
2 twelve-ounce packages chocolate chip cookies
2 packages maple syrup*
1 four-ounce package instant milk
3 two-ounce packages cream cheese*
1/2 of a .34-ounce packet lemon lime electrolyte
2 bananas
1 Hershey's bar

### Directions
Crush both packages cookies in a large spread bowl. Add both packages syrup and knead into pliable dough, just moist enough to stick together. Evenly flatten mixture into the bottom of the bowl. Starting in the center, using your knuckles, press down firmly, and work your way around the bowl, towards the outside. Dough will begin to climb sides of bowl. Work this into your pie crust, leaving about a 1½ inch lip. Smooth out when done. Dry under a fan for 1-2 hours. When dry, using a separate spread bowl, combine instant milk, cream cheese, and electrolyte and whip until smooth and creamy. Make sure all lumps/clumps are gone. Now cut up bananas and add to bowl. Mix again. Dry under a fan to dry for 3-4 hours. While drying, melt Hershey's bar and drizzle over top. Once dried, cut and serve.

* Packages of maple syrup are equal to 3 tablespoons each.
* Packages of cream cheese are equal to 4 tablespoons each.

There is more to life than cheekbones.
– Kate Winslet

# Chocolate Covered Cherry Cheesecake

Contributed by Troy Traylor

## Ingredients
2 twelve-ounce packages chocolate chip cookies
3 tablespoons hot water
1/4-pint vanilla ice cream
1 four-ounce package instant milk
2 cherry pies
1 Hershey's bar

## Directions
Crush both packages cookies in a large spread bowl. Add hot water and knead into pliable dough, just moist enough to stick together. Evenly flatten mixture out into the bottom of the spread bowl and even out. Starting in the center, using your knuckles, press down firmly, working your way around the bowl, towards the outside. Dough will begin to climb sides of bowl. Work this into your pie crust, leaving about a 1½ inch lip. Smooth out when done. Place under a fan for 1-2 hours to dry. When dry time is up, using a separate bowl, combine ice cream, instant milk, and cherry pies. Whip this until it is smooth and creamy. Takes a little work but make sure all lumps and clumps are gone. Place bowl under a fan to dry for 3-4 hours. Melt the Hershey's bar and drizzle over your cheesecake. After dry time is up, cut and serve. "Mmm Mmm Good"!

I steer my boat with hope … leaving fear astern.
– Thomas Jefferson

# Chocolate Covered Strawberry Cheesecake

Contributed by Troy Traylor

### Ingredients
1 sixteen-ounce package vanilla cream cookies
1 twelve-ounce package chocolate chip cookies
3 packages maple syrup
1 four-ounce package instant milk
3 two-ounce packages cream cheese
1 individual package nutty bars
4 tablespoons strawberry preserves
1/4 coffee mug hot chocolate mix

### Directions
Separate crème from cookies and set crème aside. Crush both packs of cookies into a fine powder in a large spread bowl. Add packages of maple syrup and knead into pliable dough, just moist enough to stick together. Once kneaded, evenly flatten into bottom of bowl. Work this into your pie crust with your knuckles, starting in the center. Leave about a 1½ inch lip. Dry under a fan for 1 hour. When crust is ready, in a separate bowl combine crème from cookies, instant milk, cream cheese, and 1 tablespoon water, then whip until smooth and creamy – no lumps or clumps. Pour into crust and even out. Crush the nutty bars and mix in bowl with the strawberry preserves. Allow cheesecake to sit under a fan for 45 minutes to form a film. Now spread the nutty bar mixture over top and sprinkle hot chocolate mixture allover. Allow this to set up for 3-4 hours. You'll write home about this one.

> The true measure of man comes in times of conflict.
>
> – Martin Luther King Jr.

# Dreamsickle Cheesecake

Contributed by Steve Pierce

### Ingredients

1 sixteen-ounce bag vanilla wafers
1 four-ounce bag instant milk
2 packages sweetener*
4 tablespoons pancake syrup
3 two-ounce packages cream cheese
1 one-ounce fruit stick (crushed)
1 packet orange electrolyte* (.34 ounce)

### Directions

Crush vanilla wafers and in a large spread bowl. Add pancake syrup and knead into pliable dough, just moist enough to stick together. Evenly flatten dough into the bottom of the bowl. Work into a crust starting in the center of bowl. Press down firmly with your knuckles and work dough around the bowl, towards the outside. Dough will climb sides of bowl. Smooth out when done. Dry under a fan for 1-2 hours. Once dry time is up, combine the remaining ingredients in a large spread bowl and whip until you have a thick and creamy consistency. Two spoons work best. You want no lumps or clumps. Takes a little work. Pour mixture inside pie crust and even out. Now place bowl back under a fan to dry for 3-4 hours. Makes 8 nice-size pieces.

*Packages of sweetener are equal to 2 tablespoons each.
*Package of electrolyte are equal to 1 tablespoon electrolyte or 4 tablespoons Kool Aid.

> The man who has never done any harm will never do any good.
> – Bernard Shaw

# Fruity Cheesecake

Contributed by Johnathan Might

### Ingredients
2 twelve-ounce packages chocolate chip cookies
3 packages Zebra cakes
3 tablespoons hot water
1 four-ounce package instant milk
3 two-ounce packages cream cheese
2 packages berry blend Kool Aid (singles)*
1·teaspoon lemon juice*

### Directions
Crush cookies and Zebra cakes in a large spread bowl. Pour in hot water and knead into pliable dough, just moist enough to stick together. Evenly flatten dough into the bottom of the bowl. Work into a crust starting in the center of bowl. Press down firmly with your knuckles and work dough around the bowl, towards the outside. Dough will climb sides of bowl. Smooth out when done. Dry under a fan 2 hour. Once dry time is up, combine remaining ingredients in a separate spread bowl and whip until you have a smooth consistency. Two spoons work best. Make sure you have no lumps or clumps. Pour milk mixture into crust and smooth out. Place bowl back under a fan to dry 4-6 hours. Cake will thicken up. Cut and serve. Simply delicious.

*Packages of Kool Aid are equal to 2 tablespoons each.
*If no access to lemon juice, melt 15 lemon candies or lemon heads in a 1/2 tablespoon hot water.

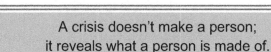

A crisis doesn't make a person;
it reveals what a person is made of.
– Warren Wiershe

# Nutty Cheesecake

Contributed by Troy Traylor

**Ingredients**
1 thirteen-ounce box graham crackers
1 four-ounce package instant milk
3 packages nutty bars
2 one-ounce chick-o-sticks
3 tablespoons hot water
3 two-ounce packages cream cheese*
3 two-ounce packages salted peanuts

**Directions**
Crush box of graham crackers in a large spread bowl. Add hot water (just enough so it sticks together) and knead into pliable dough. Evenly flatten dough into the bottom of the bowl. Work into a crust starting in the center of bowl. Press down firmly with your knuckles and work dough around the bowl, towards the outside. Dough will climb sides of bowl. Leave a 1½ inch lip and smooth out. Dry under a fan for 1-2 hours. When dry, using a separate bowl, combine instant milk, and cream cheese. Whip until you have a smooth consistency. You want no lumps or clumps. Takes a little work. Two spoons work best with whipping. Now crush your nutty bars and add to bowl. Also add the peanuts. Mix well. Pour mixture in your pie crust and dry under a fan for 3-4 hours. While it is drying crush the chick-o-sticks and sprinkle allover top of cheesecake. Once well dried, cut and serve. Your associates will appreciate you for sure.

*Packages of cream cheese are equal to 4 tablespoons each.

Trouble springs from idleness; toil from ease.
– Benjamin Franklin

# Orange Splash Cheesecake

Contributed by Troy Traylor

**Ingredients**
1 sixteen-ounce package vanilla crème cookies
1 twelve-ounce orange soda
1 four-ounce package instant milk
1 package pink lemonade* (.14 ounce)
3 two-ounce packages cream cheese*

**Directions**
Separate crème from cookies and set crème aside. Crush cookies into a fine powder in a large spread bowl. Add 4 tablespoons of soda and knead into pliable dough, just moist enough to stick together. Liquid absorption depends on brand of cookies, so you may need a little more. Once kneaded evenly flatten into the bottom of the bowl. Work into a crust starting in the center of bowl. Press down firmly with your knuckles and work dough around the bowl, towards the outside. Dough will climb sides of bowl. Leave a 1½ inch lip and smooth out. Dry under a fan for 1 hour. Once dry, in a separate bowl, combine instant milk, lemonade, cream cheese, crème from cookies, and 1 tablespoon soda and whip until all is smooth and creamy. Two spoons work best. This takes a little work but make sure all lumps and clumps are out. Once whipped, pour this mixture into pie crust and even out. Place bowl back under a fan for 3-4 more hours. Now it's time to cut and serve.

*Package of pink lemonade will be equal to 2 tablespoons.
*Packages of cream cheese are equal to 4 tablespoons each.

> " Build your adversary a golden bridge to retreat across.
> – Sun Tzu "

# The No Joke Cheesecake

Contributed by Isidro Teran

### Ingredients

1 sixteen-ounce package Duplex cookies
1 four-ounce package instant milk*
2 packages Swiss rolls
2 packages maple syrup*
3 two-ounce packages cream cheese
1 regular size package M & M's

### Directions

Separate crème from cookies and set crème aside. Crush cookies into fine powder in a spread bowl. Add maple syrup and knead into dough. Depending on brand of cookies, you may need to add a little more syrup. Make just moist enough to stick together. Evenly flatten dough in the bottom of the bowl and work into a crust, starting in the center and working towards the outside. Leave a 1½ inch lip and smooth out. Dry under a fan for 2 hours. Once dry time is up, combine instant milk, cream cheese and cookie crème in a large spread bowl and whip well. Leave no lumps or clumps. Cut Swiss rolls in half, length wise. Score dough how you will cut and place a cut Swiss roll inside each scored area. Pour milk mixture over top. Now decorate with M & M's. Place bowl back under fan to set up for 3-4 hours. Cake will stiffen up nicely. Cut into 8 nice slices. This is no joke, for sure.

*Packages of maple syrup are equal to 3 tablespoons each.
*Package: of instant milk is equal to 2/3 a 12-ounce coffee mug

> When you harbor bitterness happiness will dock elsewhere.
> – Mickey Rooney

# Section X:
# Sweets and Treats of all Kinds

# Some Cool History on Chocolate

Did you know that the cacao in chocolate is a seed (though its more commonly referred to as a bean)?

Mexico is the birthplace of chocolate; however, they contribute less than 2% of the world's cacao production. In fact, nearly 70% of the world's cacao is produced in West Africa, but sadly, many reports have found the use of child labor to be prevalent in these regions. This means that unfortunately, we've all probably eaten products of this slave-driven process.

There are three types of cacao plants, criolla, forastero, and trinitario, but most chocolate is made from the trinitario variety as this breed is the most manageable for mass production. A cacao tree needs to grow three to four years from its sapling days in order for it to be ready for harvest. During these years, the producer must prune the trees so that the trees can focus its energy on its fruit.

When I think of cacao beans, I think of something that resembles coffee beans, but raw beans straight from the fruit are originally
"goopy" and in no way dry or brown in color, and apparently, the bean taste nothing like chocolate. To begin the chocolate making process, the raw beans are put into a container to ferment for a few days. After they are perfectly fermented, they are dried in the sun for a few days. Finally, the beans are roasted then de-shelled. The resulting beans from this final stage are packed with the familiar flavor of chocolate.

Despite the long history of cacao and its indigenous use, the smooth milky chocolate bar was only invented in the 1800s. A few key developments needed to be invented first:

– 1828: A press was invented that could extract cocoa butter (the fat component) from the beans.

– 1847: It was discovered that adding additional cocoa butter to the mixture of cocoa mass made it possible to make chocolate bars.

– 1878: Conching process: a prolonged grinding of the beans improved both the texture and taste of chocolate.

Final notes: We tend to think chocolate is bad for you, but that has nothing to do with cacao. It does have a ton of sugar our bodies don't need, and vegans have beef with the milk that goes into it (pun intended). However, cacao has a ton of health benefits. It acts as an antioxidant, fighting toxins in the body and improving heart health and cholesterol control, and according to the American Cancer Institute, cacao may even help prevent cancer. When it comes down to it, cacao is actually a "superfood."

Now that you have some cool history at your disposal, time to turn the pages and get a taste or two for yourself!

# Bad Boy Brownies

Contributed by Harry Katz

## Ingredients
1 thirteen-ounce box graham crackers
1/3 of an eighteen-ounce jar peanut butter
2 two-ounce packages salted peanuts
1 four-ounce package instant milk
1 ten-ounce bag hot chocolate mix*
2 healthy handfuls raisins (optional)
1/4 coffee mug hot water

## Directions
Crush graham crackers into a fine powder in a large spread bowl. Coat with instant milk. Get any clumps out. Melt the peanut butter in the jar or an insert cup. While waiting for this to melt, combine the remaining ingredients in bowl. When peanut butter is melted, slowly pour into bowl as you stir. Consistency will get so thick it will call for you to knead with hands. Make sure this is kneaded well. Place this mixture into a large chip bag (16-ounce) and flatten out like a pizza. Cut bag open, length wise, and let dry. Overnight is best. Flavor really sets in this way. Once dry, use your ID to cut into pieces. If you cut them ID-size, you should get around 20 brownies.

*Bag of hot chocolate is equal to just shy of a 12-ounce mug.

> An open foe may prove a curse;
> but a pretended foe is worse.
> – Benjamin Franklin, *Poor Richard's Almanack*

# B's Cinnamon Rolls

Contributed by Troy Traylor

### Ingredients
1 sixteen-ounce bag vanilla wafers
4 tablespoons hot water
3 tablespoons strawberry preserves
1 handful of raisins
20 fireball candies
1 two-ounce package cream cheese
2 two-ounce packages salted peanuts

### Directions
Crush vanilla wafers in a large spread bowl and set aside. Crush fireballs as fine as possible and place in an insert cup. Add hot water and heat in a hot pot until all candies melt, about 45 minutes. Stir occasionally. Once melted, pour fireball mixture into wafer bowl and knead into dough. Once kneaded, place dough in a large sixteen-ounce chip bag and flatten. Cut bag open length wise and use a can or jar to rollout thinner. Dry for 3 hours by fan. Once dry, thoroughly mix cream cheese and strawberry preserves in a small bowl and spread over dough. Keep it about 1½ inches from the edges. Cover with lightly crush peanuts and raisins, and then carefully roll mixture into a log. Keep pressure on as you roll, and then pinch closed. Cut along the log with your ID every 1/2 to 3/4 inches, then press a bit. Let harden for 2 hours before eating. Can substitute wafers with vanilla crème cookies and use crème from cookies as icing.

Would you persuade, speak of interest, not Reason.
– Benjamin Franklin

# Chocolate Cookie Bars

Contributed by Terry Millican

### Ingredients
1 sixteen-ounce bag vanilla wafers
6 one-ounce chick-o-sticks
1 ten-ounce bag hot chocolate mix
2 two-ounce packages salted peanuts
3/4 coffee mug sunflower seeds
3-4 packages maple syrup*

### Directions
Crush vanilla wafers in a large spread bowl. Lightly crush peanuts and chick-o-sticks and mix with wafers, sunflower seeds, and hot chocolate mix. Pour in just 2 packages maple syrup and begin to knead. Keep mixture just moist enough to stick together by adding small amounts of syrup at a time. Roll mixture into a ball and place in a large sixteen-ounce chip bag. Flatten out in bag, and then cut bag open length wise and roll mixture out to about 18"x14"x1/2". Use a soda can or condiment jar as rolling pin. Let this sit overnight, under a fan, so flavor will set in (fan also keeps any bugs off). When ready, use your ID and cut pieces about ID size. Should get about 16.

*Packages of maple syrup are equal to 3 tablespoons each.

Face your deficiencies and acknowledge them; but do not let them master you. Let them teach you patience, sweetness, insight.
– Helen Keller (1880-1968)

# Crazy Cookie Rolls

Contributed by Troy Traylor

### Ingredients
1 sixteen-ounce package Duplex crème cookies
3 two-ounce packages cream cheese
3/4 coffee mug hot chocolate mix
5 tablespoons hot water
1 two-ounce package salted peanuts
1 heaping tablespoon peanut butter

### Directions
Separate crème from cookies and set crème aside. Crush cookies into fine powder in a large spread bowl. Add cream cheese and knead into thick, pliable dough. Roll into a ball, put in a large 16-ounce chip bag, and then flatten. Cut bag open and use a soda can or jar to roll mixture thin, approximately a 1/4 inch thick. Let sit while you make the icing. In an insert cup, combine hot chocolate mix, hot water, and stir well. Place insert cup in a hot pot for 20 minutes to melt some. While waiting, lightly crush peanuts and set aside. Now add crème from cookies and the peanut butter to insert cup. Stir and place back in hot pot for 1 hour. Stir occasionally. Once cooked, carefully roll cookie mixture into a log. Press down firmly as you roll to keep tight. Use your ID to cut pieces about 1/2-3/4-inch-thick along the log. Layout pieces on plastic and press down to partially flatten. Remove icing from hot pot and pour over the cookie rolls. Now sprinkle peanuts over all. Allow to sit for 2 hours before you eat. Flavors will blend.

66

The greatest accomplishment is not in never failing,
but in rising up after you fall.
– Vince Lombardi

99

# Crème Pie-Caliente'

Contributed by Troy Traylor

**Ingredients**
1 sixteen-ounce box oatmeal crème pies
6 jalapeno peppers (1.3-ounce singles)

**Directions**
Split oatmeal crème pies in half using your ID card. Cut jalapeno peppers in half, length wise and de-seed. Put a slice of jalapeno on each half and top with other half. You will be amazed at how good this is. *A must try!*

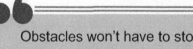 Obstacles won't have to stop you. If you run into a wall, don't turn around and give up. Figure out how to climb it, go through it, or work around it.
– Michael Jordan

# French Banana Pudding

Contributed by Troy Traylor

## Ingredients

1 sixteen-ounce bag vanilla wafers
1 four-ounce bag instant milk
1/4 coffee mug hot water
5 bananas
1/2 coffee mug French cappuccino (powder)

## Directions

Crush vanilla wafers into fine powder and place in a large spread bowl. Dice bananas into small pieces. Now combine remaining ingredients in this spread bowl and mix well. Two spoons work best. You want a smooth consistency without any lumps or clumps. Place bowl aside for 2 hours so mixture stiffens up a bit.

> Adversity is like a strong wind.
> It tears away from us all but the things that cannot be torn,
> so that we see ourselves as we really are.
> – Arthur Golden

# G-Wiz

Contributed by Joseph Garcia

**Ingredients**
1 Snicker's bar
1 large-honey bun
1 brownie (single package)
1 tablespoon peanut butter

**Directions**
Place Snicker's bar in a hot pot until fully melted, approximately 20 minutes. Right before candy bar is melted, press brownie flat. Now coat honey bun with peanut butter and top with brownie. Remove Snicker's bar from hot pot and pour over brownie. Allow it to cool or eat it hot – either way is just as good.

 Failure is a great teacher and if you're open to it, every mistake has a lesson to offer.
– Oprah Winfrey

# Mexican Brownies

Contributed by Isidro Teran

### Ingredients
1 sixteen-ounce package Duplex crème cookies
5 fireball candies
1 six-ounce bag sunflower seeds
2 two-ounce packages energy mix
1 sixteen-ounce bag vanilla wafers
1 ten-ounce bag hot chocolate mix*
2 two-ounce packages salted peanuts
1/2 coffee mug hot water

### Directions
Separate crème from cookies and set crème aside. Crush cookies and vanilla wafers and divide evenly between two bowls. Crush fireball candies as fine as possible and set aside. Equally divide hot chocolate mix, sunflower seeds, peanuts and energy mix between the bowls. Mix well and pour a 1/4 coffee mug hot water in each bowl and knead thoroughly. Combine both mixtures and place in a large sixteen-ounce chip bag. Flatten out evenly in the bag, cut open length wise and allow to dry overnight. The next day, combine crème from cookies, fireballs, and 2 tablespoons hot water in an insert cup and heat in a hot pot, unstirred, for 30 minutes. Remove insert, stir well, and heat another 30 minutes. Once heated, whip well and pour over brownies. Allow this to dry for 1 hour before you cut. You can cut about 16 pieces from this.

*Bag of hot chocolate mix is equal to a lite 12-ounce coffee mug.

> We all need lots of powerful long-range goals to help us past the short-term obstacles. – Jim Rohn

# Penana-Banana Pudding

Contributed by Troy Traylor, Jr.

## Ingredients

4-6 bananas
1 sixteen-ounce bag vanilla wafers*
1 four-ounce bag instant milk
1/4 coffee mug hot water
1 tablespoon cinnamon (from kitchen or flavored oatmeal)

## Directions

This is a real easy recipe, and you will love the results. Cut the bananas into small pieces and crush the vanilla wafers. Place all crushed wafers, banana pieces, instant milk, and hot water into a large spread bowl and stir well. It is best to use two spoons as you whip. Continue to whip until you get the consistency you desire. Make sure all the milk is dissolved. Set bowl aside for 30-45 minutes to thicken up. If it gets too thick just add a spoon of hot water at a time till you have the pudding texture. Once this thickens, sprinkle with your cinnamon and mix well. Unless you're real hungry, you might want to invite a friend. Truly delicious!!

*Vanilla crème cookies can be used instead of vanilla wafers, but wafers are best. If you do use crème cookies, you do not have to separate the crème, but do crush finely.

Blaming is a futile exercise –
yelling at darkness doesn't make it light.
– C. Swindoll

# Peanut Butter Cups

Contributed by Troy Traylor

**Ingredients**
1 sixteen-ounce package Duplex crème cookies
1 Hershey's bar (regular size)
2 ½ packages maple syrup*
2 tablespoons peanut butter
1 two-ounce package salted peanuts

**Directions**
Separate crème from cookies and set crème aside. Crush cookies into fine powder in a large spread bowl. Dice Hershey's bar into tiny pieces and add to bowl with 2 packages syrup. Knead into pliable dough, just moist enough to stick together. Once kneaded divide dough and roll into balls. Use your thumb and press a dent into each ball. These are your cups. Allow to dry for 1 hour. While waiting, combine crème from cookies, peanut butter, and remaining syrup in an insert cup and whip. Place insert in a hot pot to heat while cups are drying. Stir occasionally. Once cups are dry, remove insert from hot pot, stir and spoon mixture into cups. Crush up your peanuts and sprinkle over your peanut butter cups. Allow these to sit another 45 minutes to 1 hour before you serve. Simply delicious!

*Packages of syrup are equal to 3 tablespoons each.

> It would be great if people never got angry at someone for doing something, they've done themselves.
> – Rodney Dangerfield

# Taffy Dayz

Contributed by Robert Dawson

**Ingredients**
2 four-ounce packages creamer (powder)
2 packages orange electrolyte* (.34 ounces each)
1 package lemon lime electrolyte*(.34 ounce)
1/4 coffee mug hot water

**Directions**
In a large spread bowl combine instant milk and electrolytes. Mix and slowly begin to add hot water. Whip (two spoons are best for this) until all lumps are gone. Mixture will get stiff and sticky. Use hands to continue and fold the mixture into itself. Once all is kneaded well, spread out some plastic on bunk and roll mixture out into a long rope type. Make string-thin. Allow mixture to dry for 6-8 hours. You will not believe how good this is.

*Packages of electrolyte are equal to 1 tablespoon electrolyte or 4 tablespoons Kool Aid each.

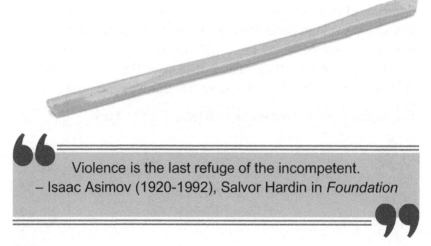

66
Violence is the last refuge of the incompetent.
– Isaac Asimov (1920-1992), Salvor Hardin in *Foundation*
99

# TJ's Peanut Butter Squares

Contributed by Troy Traylor, Jr.

### Ingredients
3/4 coffee mug sugar
3/4 coffee mug hot water
1 eighteen-ounce jar peanut butter
2 four-ounce packages instant milk
1 sixteen-ounce package Duplex crème cookies

### Directions
In a large spread bowl combine sugar, instant milk, and hot water. Stir until all is dissolved. Pour liquid in a rice bag and place bag in a hot pot to heat for 30 minutes. Stir occasionally to reach a thick and sticky consistency. While heating, crush cookies with crème inside and melt peanut butter in its jar. When milk mixture is ready, combine all ingredients in a large spread bowl and knead well. It takes some work but make sure all is mixed well. Place mixture in a large sixteen-ounce chip bag and flatten out. Cut chip bag down the center and open. Allow mixture to sit overnight so the flavors soak in and the mixture stiffens up. Cut ID size when ready. You can melt a Hershey's bar and drizzle over top if you want or eat as is. M & M's are also a nice addition. Don't be afraid to experiment.

To choose one's attitude in a given set of circumstances is to choose one's own way.
— Victor Frankl

# Conversion Chart

## Liquid Measurements

| Gallons | Quarts | Pints | Cups | Fluid Ounces |
|---------|--------|-------|------|--------------|
| 1 gal. | 4 qt. | 8 pt. | 16 cups | 128 fl.oz. |
| 1/2 gal. | 2 qt. | 4 pt. | 8 cups | 64 fl. oz. |
| 1/4 gal. | 1 qt. | 2 pt. | 4 cups | 32 fl. oz. |
| 1/8 gal. | 1/2 qt. | 1 pt. | 2 cups | 16 fl. oz. |
| 1/16 gal. | 1/4 qt. | 1/2 pt. | 1 cup | 8 fl. oz. |

## Dry Measurements

| Cups | Tablespoons | Teaspoons | Ounces | Grams |
|------|-------------|-----------|--------|-------|
| 1 cup | 16 tbsp. | 48 tsp. | 8 oz. | 229 g. |
| 3/4 cup | 12 tbsp. | 36 tsp. | 6 oz. | 171 g. |
| 2/3 cup | 10⅔ tbsp. | 32 tsp. | 5.34 oz. | 152 g. |
| 1/2 cup | 8 tbsp. | 24 tsp. | 4 oz. | 114 g. |
| 1/3 cup | 5⅓ tbsp. | 16 tsp. | 2.67 oz. | 76 g. |
| 1/4 cup | 4 tbsp. | 12 tsp. | 2 oz. | 57 g. |
| 1/8 cup | 2 tbsp. | 6 tsp. | 1 oz. | 29 g. |
| 1/16 cup | 1 tbsp. | 3 tsp. | .5 oz. | 14 g. |

# Your Shopping List

## All the ingredients for the recipes in this book

I have attempted to make your culinary journey easier for you. I realize that sizes may differ from state to state. I have listed the actual sizes for all products, and also broken many measurements down to coffee mugs, teaspoons, or tablespoons. The coffee mug sizes are measured using a 12-ounce coffee mug. Tablespoons are the commissary-purchased spoon at my facility, which are fairly standard. Now a teaspoon is basically half of the commissary-purchased spoon. I hope this makes it easier for you.

All you have to do now is find the recipe of your liking, mark the ingredients on your commissary slip, and wait until your next commissary. This, of course, is much easier for those of you on the outside; all you have to do is add the ingredients to your grocery list or shopping cart. Either way, I hope you enjoy your journey, and love the results.

*Candy/Pastries*

| | |
|---|---|
| Bagels | Single/Regular Size |
| Candy Bars | Regular Size |
| Cherry Pies | 4 oz. (4" x 2" Box) |
| Chick-o-Sticks | 1 oz. Single |
| Fireballs | 10 oz. Bag |
| Fruit/Mint Sticks | 1 oz. Single |
| M & M's | Regular Size |
| Orange Slices | 10.25 oz. Bag |

*Chips/Crackers*

| | |
|---|---|
| Bacon Potato Skins Chips | 8 oz. Bag |
| BBQ Chips | 8 oz. Bag |
| Cheese and Chive Crackers | 1.375 oz. Package |

| | |
|---|---|
| Cheese Curls | 3 oz. Bag |
| Cheese Puffs | 11 oz. Bag |
| Cheetos | 3 oz. Bag |
| Chili Cheese Fritos | 16 oz. Bag |
| Corn Chips | 16 oz. Bag |
| Doritos | 3 oz. Bag |
| Graham Crackers | 13 oz. Box |
| Jalapeno Chips | 8 oz. Bag |
| Nacho Chips | 3 oz. Bag |
| Party Mix | 11 oz. Bag |
| Pork Skins | 2.75 oz. Bag |
| Regular Potato Chips | 3 oz. Bag |
| Salsa Verde Chip | 3 oz. Bag |
| Saltine Crackers | 4 Sleeve Box |
| Shabang Chips/Salt and Vinegar Chips | 8 oz. Bag |
| Snack Crackers | 13.7 oz. (4 Sleeves) |
| Tortilla Chips | 16 oz. Bag |

*Condiments*

| | |
|---|---|
| Back Country Chorizo | 11.25 oz. |
| BBQ Sauce | 18 oz. Bottle |
| Butter-Sticks/Bowl | 4 oz./Bowls Vary |
| Chili Garlic Sauce | 8 oz. Bottle |
| Cinnamon | |
| Corn Starch | |
| Cream Cheese | 2 oz. Packages |
| French Onion Dip | Homemade |
| Grape Jelly | 12 oz. Bottle |
| Habanera Sauce | 8 oz. Bottle |
| Honey | 8 oz. Bottle |
| Hot Sauce | 8 oz. Bottle |
| Jalapeno Pepper Singles | 1.3 oz. Package |
| Jalapeno Pepper Slices | .6 oz./.7 oz. Pack |
| Ketchup | 20 oz. Bottle |
| Lemon Juice | |
| Lowry Seasoned Salt | 1.75 oz. Bottle |
| Maple Syrup | 3 tbsp. packs |

| | |
|---|---|
| Mayonnaise | 15 oz. Bottle |
| Mustard | 14 oz Bottle |
| Old Fashioned Cream Cheese | 2 oz. Packages |
| Old Fashioned Ranch Dressing | 2 oz. Packages |
| Onion Flakes/Onion Powder/Garlic Powder | 1. 75 oz. Bottles |
| Parmesan Cheese | 1.75 oz. Bottle |
| Peanut Butter | 18 oz. Jar |
| Pickle | 9 oz. Package |
| Ranch Dressing | 1.5 oz. Packets |
| Relish | 8 oz. Jar |
| Salad Dressing | 15 oz. Jar |
| Salsa | 8 oz. Bottle |
| Salt/Black Pepper Shakers | Disposal Shakers |
| Sandwich Spread | 15 oz. Bottle/Jar |
| Seasoning Packet from Ramen | Single Package |
| Shredded Mozzarella Cheese | |
| Soy Sauce | 5 oz. Bottle |
| Squeeze Cheese | 16 oz. Bottle |
| Strawberry Preserves | 12 oz. Bottle |
| Sugar Cubes | 1 tsp. each |
| Sweeteners | Single Packages |
| Taco Seasoning | 1.5 oz. Bag |
| Teriyaki Marinade | |
| Vegetable Oil | |
| Velveeta Queso Blanco | 4 oz. Tub |
| White Pepper | Bottle/can |
| Worcestershire Sauce | |

*Cookies*

| | |
|---|---|
| Chocolate Chip | 12 oz. Package |
| Duplex/Vanilla/Strawberry Crème | 16 oz. Package |
| Maria Cookies | 5.6 oz. Package |
| Vanilla Wafers | 16 oz. Bag |

*Drinks*

| | |
|---|---|
| Electrolyte Drink Mix | .34 oz. Packets |
| French Vanilla Cappuccino | 12 oz. Bag |
| French Vanilla Creamer | 12 oz. Bag |

| | |
|---|---|
| Hot Chocolate Mix | 10 oz. Bag |
| Iced Tea Mix | .14 oz. Packet |
| Instant Milk | 4 oz. Bag |
| Juices/Sodas | 12 oz. Can |
| Kool Aid/Lemonade Mix | .14 oz. Packet |

### Little Debbie's

| | |
|---|---|
| Brownies | Single Packs |
| Honey Buns (Box) | 16 oz. Box of 12 |
| Honey Buns (Singles) | Large Size Singles |
| Nutty Bars | 12 oz. Box of 6 |
| Oatmeal Crème Pies | 16 oz. Box of 12 |
| Zebra Cakes | 12 oz. Box of 6 |

### Meats

| | |
|---|---|
| Back Country Buffalo Chicken with Sauce | 5 oz. Package |
| BBQ Beef | 11.25 oz. Package |
| Beef Stew | 11.25 oz. Package |
| Beef Tips | 8 oz. Box |
| Boneless Chicken Thighs | Misc. Weight |
| Chicken Breast | Misc. Weight |
| Chicken Chunks | 7 oz. Package |
| Chicken Quarters | Misc. Weight |
| Chili With/Without Beans | 11.25 oz. Package |
| Crawfish | 1/2 Pound |
| Fish Steaks | 3.5 oz. Package |
| Hot Dogs | 4-any size |
| Mackerel | 3.5 oz. Package |
| Mexican Beef | 8 oz. Package |
| Pepperoni Slices | 3.5 oz. Package |
| Pickled Sausage | 5 oz. Package |
| Sardines | 3.53 oz. Package |
| Sliced Salami | 4 Slices |
| Sliced Sweet Ham | 4 Slices |
| Sliced Turkey | 4 Slices |
| Spam | 3 oz. Package |
| Summer Sausage | 5 oz. Package |
| Tuna | 4.23 oz. Package |

| | |
|---|---|
| Turkey Bites | 4 oz. Package |
| Vienna Sausage | 3 oz. Package |

*Miscellaneous*

| | |
|---|---|
| Bananas | 1 Bunch |
| Bell Peppers | Large/Small |
| Black Olives | 1/2 Coffee Mug |
| Bread | Loaf |
| Brown Gravy | .75 oz. Package Mix |
| Celery | 1 Stalk |
| Coriander Leaves | Just a Few |
| Corn Tortillas | 10 oz. Package |
| Cream of Celery Soup | 10 oz. can |
| Cream of Mushroom Soup | 10 oz. can |
| Dehydrated Mushrooms/Vegetables | 3 oz. Package |
| Energy/Trail Mix | 2 oz. Package |
| Flour Tortillas | 10 oz. Package |
| Hard Boiled Eggs | Just a Few |
| Instant Black Beans | 10 oz.-16 oz. Bag |
| Instant Chili Beans | 12 oz. Bag |
| Instant Oatmeal | 10 Package Box |
| Instant Potatoes | 10 oz. Bag |
| Instant Rice – Brown | 6.5 oz. Bag |
| Instant Rice – White | 8 oz. Bag |
| Jalapeno Cheddar Cheese | 4 oz. Tub |
| Jambalaya Mix | 8.8 oz. Box |
| Lettuce | 1 Head |
| Mozzarella Cheese Sticks | Single Serving Pack |
| Onions | Large/Small |
| Pecans | To taste |
| Pepper Jack Cheese Sticks | Single Serving Pack |
| Potatoes | Misc. |
| Raisins | To taste |
| Ramen Noodles | 3 oz. Packages |
| Refried Beans | 15 oz. Bag |
| Salted Peanuts | 2 oz. Bags |
| Sesame Seeds | To taste |

| | |
|---|---|
| Shredded Cheddar Cheese | To taste |
| Spring Onions | Small |
| Sunflower Seeds | 6 oz. Package |
| Sweet Potatoes | 4 Large |
| Tomatoes | 3 Large |
| Tostadas | 1 Package |
| Vegetables from Tray | 4 oz. Servings |
| Whole Wheat Cereal | 36 oz. |

Total Ingredients – 157 Items

# Closing

I would like to take a moment and sincerely thank each and every person that has purchased, read, and shared this book. It is truly a beautiful thing in today's world to see people helping people, helping people.

In this closing, I would like to share with you my view on becoming free from the prison you may find yourself in. Not all "prisons" have bars. Many of us are physically in prison, but many more are in a mental prison of sorts; the result is basically the same. We can allow this experience to be memorable, or we can allow this experience to be miserable. It is a choice, and as humans we are free to choose.

For me, I know that Jesus died for my Salvation, and He makes the power of His death and Resurrection present to me. I set all my hope on the grace that Jesus brings to my life. Salvation is my life's journey.

It is both my hope and my prayer that you know we have all been saved by Jesus in the sense that through His life, death, and resurrection, Jesus has done everything necessary to bring us to heaven. But we must, in our turn, freely stay united to Jesus by both faith and good works. With this, Salvation can be our journey.

May God bless you and your loved ones in all you, and they, do.

Prayerfully,

Troy Neal Traylor, Sr.

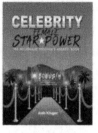

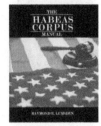

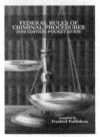

Troy Traylor

Made in the USA
Las Vegas, NV
07 December 2021

36457950R00128